EFFECTIVE PRESENTATIONS

John Kirkman

Guidelines
for giving
EFFECTIVE PRESENTATIONS

Tactics and techniques
for talking
to large or small groups

Ramsbury Books
on technical communication

Published by
Ramsbury Books
Address for orders: PO Box 106, Marlborough, Wiltshire SN8 2RU.

© John Kirkman 1994

All rights reserved. No part of this book
may be reproduced in any form by any electronic or mechanical means
(including photocopying, recording, or information storage and retrieval)
without permission in writing from the publishers.

First edition 1994

ISBN 0 9521762 1 1

British Library Cataloguing-in-Publication Data
A catalogue record for this book is available
from the British Library

Ramsbury Books is a business name of
the John Kirkman Communication Consultancy
Partners: John and Susan Kirkman
Witcha Cottage
Ramsbury
Marlborough
Wiltshire
SN8 2HQ

Printed and bound in the UK by the Ashford Press, Southampton

CONTENTS

	Page
About this book	x
About the author	xi
Acknowledgements	xii
A note on 'audience'	xii

Chapter 1 Before we get down to detail   1

Can you become a good speaker by reading a book?	1
The arrangement of the book	4

Chapter 2 Analysing your aim, audience and context   7

The need to be selective	7
Analysing your aim(s)	8
Analysing your audience	9
Analysing the context	13

Chapter 3 Assembling material for your talk   15

Creating an outline	15
Which structure?	16
Giving focus and stimulating ideas	17

Chapter 4 Deciding how to start   21

Building confidence by starting well	21
What is required for a 'good start'	22
Aiding motivation	23
Catching and holding attention	25
Establishing your credentials	29
Aiding orientation	31

Contents (continued) Page

        Should you keep people guessing?   32
        Should you begin with a story or assertion?   32
        Ten attention-getting devices   33
        How NOT to start   35

Chapter 5 Organising the middle of your presentation   37

        Deciding proportions of time   37
        Possible ways of organising the main body   38
        A strategy for describing and explaining   41
        The 'unloading rate' for your information   43
        Short-term and long-term memory   44
        Use of visual aids   46

Chapter 6 Bringing the talk to a conclusion   47

Chapter 7 Preparing your notes   51

        Need for notes   51
        Using your aids as notes   53
        How to prepare notes   55
        Why not use a full script?   55
        'Thinking through'   58
        Reminders about visual aids   58
        Indications of time   59
        Being prepared to adjust your plan   60
        Length   63
        Size and layout   64
        To hold or not to hold?   66

Chapter 8 Deciding whether to use visual aids   69

        How visual aids help you and your audience   69
        Help in dealing with numbers   70
        Help in dealing with objects or processes   70

Contents (continued)   **Page**

Help in dealing with abstractions	71
A caveat: visual images need a verbal frame	72
Help in varying the mode of your presentation	74
Help in reinforcing and consolidating your message	75
Should you use visual aids all the time?	76

Chapter 9   Deciding which visual-aid equipment to use   79

Factors that influence your choice	79
When to create your visual materials	82
Using more than one type of visual-aid equipment	84
Advantages and disadvantages of common types of equipment	84
Chalkboards and whiteboards	85
Flip-charts	87
Overhead projectors	89
Prepared large-scale sheets	94
Physical models or samples	96
Handouts	98
35mm-slide projectors	112
Filmstrips and films	117
Videotapes	118
Closed-circuit television	120
Audio aids	121
Multi-media	122

Chapter 10   Handling visual-aid equipment   123

The need for foresight	123
Viewing and arranging the room	123
Choosing where to stand	126
Pointing	129
Leading with words	131

Contents (continued)   **Page**

            Handling the overhead projector   133
            Word:image mismatching   134

Chapter 11   General advice on designing 'visual' material for use in presentations   137

            General advice   137
            Statement visuals and illustration visuals   138
            Controlling your audience's reading of your visual   140
            The visual impact of words and numbers   141
            Avoiding overload   143
            Meeting your audience's expectations   146
            Tables   148
            Bar charts   148
            Circular ('Pie') charts   150
            Line charts (graphs)   151
            Flow charts and block diagrams   151

Chapter 12   Dealing with nervousness   153

            Understanding the causes and effects of nervousness   153
            Why were you asked to speak to a group?   154
            What are you really afraid of?   155

Chapter 13   Delivering the presentation   159

            Doing simple things well   159
            Standing up straight   159
            What to do with your hands   161
            Movement   161
            Speaking comprehensibly and clearly   162
            Over-all policy for choosing language   163

Contents (continued)   **Page**

Use of jargon	163
'Plain English'	164
Speaking to multi-national audiences	164
Fillers	166
Clarity of diction and variety of intonation	167
Maintaining eye-contact	168
Level of formality	169
Dealing with questions	170
Rehearsing	171
Preparing a 'Plan B'	173

Appendix   175

Check-lists for evaluating presentations	175
Criteria related to content	175
Criteria related to delivery	177

About this book

My aim in this book is to offer help with the types of 'presentations' increasingly required in professional life: not presentations of gifts as leaving presents; rather, talks to large or small groups, in which you present or seek information for commercial, industrial, research, or governmental activities. I exclude conversations, discussion meetings, interviews, and 'sales' presentations. My topic is the type of descriptive, explanatory, or persuasive presentation an individual (or a team) is asked to prepare and present to several others. The setting may be formal or informal: but always, a *speaker* has to stand up before an audience and 'give a talk'.

John Kirkman
Ramsbury
Wiltshire
January, 1994

About the author

John Kirkman was formerly Director of the Communication Studies Unit at the University of Wales Institute of Science and Technology, Cardiff (now University of Wales, College of Cardiff), UK. Since 1983, he was worked full-time as a consultant on scientific and technical communication. He has consulted for more than 250 organisations in 16 countries.

He has been a Visiting Lecturer in Technical Communication at the University of Michigan, USA, and at the Massachusetts Institute of Technology, USA, and a Visiting Fellow in Linguistics at Princeton University, USA. He has published more than 70 articles, and has written, edited or contributed to 10 books, including *Effective Writing* (with Christopher Turk, Spon, 1989), *Good Style: writing for science and technology* (Spon, 1992), and *Full Marks: advice on punctuation for scientific and technical writing* (Ramsbury Books, 1993). The Society for Technical Communication (USA) gave him its Outstanding Article Award in 1974, and an Award for Distinguished Technical Communication (shared with Peter Hunt) in 1987.

The John Kirkman Communication Consultancy specialises in training writers and editors. It also offers research and development in scientific and technical communication, reviewing and editing of technical documentation, and advice on recruitment of technical communicators.

Acknowledgements

I am grateful for permission to reproduce the following materials:

> For illustrations in Figures 1, 5 and 6:
> Fokker Aircraft BV, Amsterdam, Holland

> For illustrations in Figures 2a and 2b:
> Danfoss A/S, Nordborg, Denmark

A note on 'audience'

Some enthusiasts for 'correct' English will be upset by my use of plural pronouns and verbs with the collective noun *audience*. However, it seemed strange to write:

> '... face the audience, and involve *it* all in the interaction',

Accordingly, I chose to consider the audience as a plural entity on most occasions throughout the book:

> '... face the audience, and involve them all in the interaction.'

In doing that, I have the support of the authoritative *A Comprehensive Grammar of the English Language* (Quirk R, Greenbaum S, Leech G, and Svartvik J, Longman 1989, page 316), which comments that the difference in use of singular and plural nouns reflects:

> 'a difference in point of view: the singular stresses the nonpersonal collectivity of the group, and the plural stresses the personal individuality within the group.'

Since I want to stress the importance of considering the audience as a collection of individuals, not as a single mass — 'them' — it seemed particularly appropriate to use plural pronouns and verbs.

CHAPTER 1

Before we get down to detail

Can you become a good speaker by reading a book?

Can you become a good speaker just by reading a book? Probably not: but you *can* learn from a book the strategies and tactics that will enable you to present yourself and your information competently and comfortably.

Learning to make effective presentations has much in common with learning to swim or to drive a car. In all three learning processes, I found the main difficulty at first was co-ordination.

In swimming, I found it difficult to remember what to do with my arms, what to do with my legs, how to hold my head, and to breathe, *all at the same time*! During my early efforts at car-driving, I wondered if I would ever co-ordinate smoothly my efforts to press down the accelerator gradually + allow the clutch to rise slowly + gradually release the handbrake + indicate that I was about to pull out into the traffic + look in my rear-view mirror + look carefully ahead to see that the road was clear + listen to the engine to check whether it was racing or was about to stall + hold the steering wheel firmly at the 'ten-to-two' position + pray! It seems similarly daunting, as you learn to address audiences, to have to concentrate not only on what you want to say but also on how to stand, how to speak, and how to handle visual aids. Be reassured. With practice, co-ordination comes.

A few people may become spell-binding political orators or gloriously entertaining after-dinner speakers: most of us will not. But this book is not aimed at producing a few outstanding performers. No doubt most of you are content with being able to swim comfortably and safely; you are not aiming to win an

Olympic medal. No doubt most of you are content to be able to drive comfortably and reliably: you are not aiming to become a champion racing driver. I assume that in studying effective speaking, you are aiming primarily at basic competence: if outstanding talent develops, that will be a bonus. So this book offers sound tactics and techniques that will make you comfortable, confident, and successful in presenting yourself and your information in various contexts.

Different personalities react variously to the task of marshalling just the right information to produce just the required response from an audience. For some, there will always be an element of stress in addressing an audience. But we know now that it is possible to live with stress, to manage it, and to reduce it. Over the years, on courses on effective speaking, I have been delighted to watch the change in large numbers of people who were at first petrified by the idea of having to give a talk. For the most part, they brought about the change in themselves. They changed their attitude to the business of speaking to an audience. They came to understand the pressures and difficulties in effective speaking. By analysing what goes on in the activity of speaking, they drew insights into how to reduce stress and control anxiety. They took a firmer command of their information and their audiences. With practice, they came to know the satisfaction of giving controlled and competent presentations.

I have now used the qualification 'with practice' twice. I want to stress that you will need to practise if you are to develop skill in making presentations. Certainly, this book can help by guiding your analysis of what happens when we communicate. It can help by suggesting tactics for handling your information, and by advising you how to deliver your talk. Also, you can learn a great deal by watching other speakers closely, and noting the devices that work well (or badly!) in their presentations. But as with swimming, we can develop our own skill only by trying it out.

Most of us, during the learning process, experience the equivalent of some involuntary intakes of swimming-pool water! For that reason, I strongly recommend that you practise, if possible, in the friendly environment of a short course or training programme. There, all learners are in the same situation; everyone is supportive; it does not matter if things go wrong — though in my experience they rarely do. Of course, you cannot expect to be transformed in one or two days: but if the talks you give during practice sessions are simulations of 'real-life' tasks, they can help you learn the tactics you will need for tackling those tasks in your daily work. When you come to give similar talks in real life, it will be reassuring to know that you have used the necessary tactics successfully during your training.

The most valuable aspect of a course is that you can get feedback from other learners, from advisors, and from videotapes of your presentations. Self-appraisal, reflection after a talk on 'how it went', is essential; but inevitably, you are influenced by your own awareness of what you were trying to do and how you felt at the time. It is valuable to hear from other people what *they* thought you were trying to do, and how you sounded and looked *to them*. It is also very enlightening to see yourself on videotape: it is not quite the same person as you see in the bathroom mirror!

I know, however, that many of you will not be able to attend a course. So I have made this book as practical as possible. Much is presented in check-list form, so that when time is short you can find your way quickly to a succinct review of the points you should cover in your planning and preparation. The check-lists of things to consider have been tried out thoroughly over the years, but if you find any gaps, please let me know.

The arrangement of the book

Newcomers to the business of presentation-giving often worry too much about 'elocution' — putting on a 'standard English' accent — and having a good platform presence. Of course, it is important to speak clearly and to look comfortable; but more important than either of those qualities is control over subject-matter. Over many years, I have asked hundreds of students what impresses them most about good speakers. Their comments have been virtually unanimous: 'The most important thing is that they obviously know their subjects and present them in ways that we can understand'.

Speakers who obviously have a firm grasp of their subjects, and who present their information cogently and clearly — these command the confidence and respect of audiences. Speakers whose lack of preparation causes them to fumble for the next point, to fumble for words, and to fumble among a pile of transparencies beside an overhead projector — these create a sense of embarrassment and unease in their audiences, which soon turns to impatience and resentment.

So, planning what information to use in a talk, and how to arrange it must come before considerations of delivery. But before you can begin planning, it is necessary to know the answers to the following questions:

- What is the aim of giving the talk?
- Who will be in the audience?
- What will be the context:
    - the technical/social/'political' situation?
    - the physical venue for the talk?
    - the constraints of time and equipment?

The arrangement of the book 5

So Chapter 2 discusses those questions. Then, Chapters 3 to 6 discuss how to select and arrange the content of your talk. Chapter 7 advises you to support yourself with carefully prepared notes. Chapters 8 to 11 discuss the selection and handling of visual aids. And Chapters 12 and 13 give advice on delivering your talk.

At the end, an Appendix contains check-lists for evaluating presentations. You may find those check-lists useful, too, to guide you through the questions you ought to ask as you review your plans for your own presentations.

CHAPTER 2

Analysing your aim, audience and context

The need to be selective

When you make a presentation in professional life, your aim is rarely to tell the audience everything you know about a subject. Usually, you must select, from all that *could* be presented, just the items and details that will be of interest and use to your audience.

'Real-life' situations usually contrast strongly with the situation that exists when you make presentations in academic settings. In academic settings, you are normally asked to make a presentation for *your* benefit. In 'real life', you are normally asked to make a presentation for the benefit of *the audience*.

In academic settings, your main motive is to display. You aim to show a teacher, who usually knows more than you do about the subject, how much knowledge you have assembled and assimilated. Your main objective is to gain credit (usually, to score marks). You aim to show the breadth and depth of the knowledge you have acquired, to demonstrate that you understand how it has been derived, and to show that you can use it in standard situations. In 'real' life, you are seldom engaged in that sort of mark-scoring activity. Certainly, you normally want your presentation to bring you credit, respect, credibility, and perhaps promotion. That is a very reasonable *part* objective; but it should rarely be the *principal* objective. Normally, in a presentation in business, industry, research, or government, *your* job is to put other people in a position to do *their* jobs — to provide them with the information they need to take decisions, make plans, arrange manufacturing or administrative activity, or operate processes or procedures. You gain or lose credit by the accuracy, clarity, economy, propriety, and consideration with which you do that. In those circumstances, it is rarely appropriate to present everything you know: *selecting* becomes a key activity — choosing the items, from all that could be presented, that will be directly relevant to the interests and needs of your audience.

Before you can choose, you must identify clearly those interests and needs. That is why, in the first stage of your preparation for a talk, you must go through check-lists of questions about the aim, audience, and context of the presentation.

Analysing your aim(s)

What am I trying to do in this presentation? Note that this is not the same question as 'What is my topic?'. You know that your topic is a product, a process, or an idea. You are asking yourself now about the aim of making the presentation:

- Why am I preparing this talk?
- What am I trying to achieve for myself, and/or for the audience?
- What response do I want from this audience?
- What do they want and/or expect from me?

Of course, you may have a combination of aims. You may decide that you have to fulfil two or more of the communication tasks listed in the box on the facing page. It is important, though, to identify your aim(s) clearly, and not (for example) to wander off into irrelevant *description* and *explanation* of components when your aim should be to *instruct* your audience how to operate a piece of equipment or a process.

> A list of possible communication aims:
>
> - to describe (to focus on *what*);
>
> - to explain (to focus on *how* and/or *why*);
>
> - to instruct (to focus on *what the reader must do*);
>
> - to specify (to focus on the *obligations* that will lie on the reader);
>
> - to evaluate and recommend (to focus on *what you think*);
>
> - to persuade (to focus on *what you want* and *why the audience should want it, too*);
>
> - to provoke ideas, to 'brainstorm' (to *stir up* as many ideas as possible without judgement or selection);
>
> - to establish/re-establish/repair relationships prior to other activities, to emphasise the diplomatic/social/political aspects of a business or technical interaction.
>
> - . . . .

Analysing your audience

As you think about your audience, beware of the tendency to see them as a group — 'them'. When you are a speaker, it is tempting to think of the audience as a single entity, making a collective response; but when you are in an audience yourself, you feel and respond mainly as an individual. So, as you prepare your talk, think of yourself as addressing many individuals.

Of course, members of an audience may have a sense of being part of several groups: of a random group assembled for the talk, of a special-subject group, of a racial group, of a sexual group, of a group with political/social/industrial loyalties. But even if we are in the same audience, the intellectual and emotional responses that are triggered in *my* head and heart are not exactly the same as are triggered in *yours*. I suspect that, like me, you respond most favourably to speakers who seem to have considered just *my* interests and problems. That is why, as you make choices of what to say and how to say it, it is essential to think hard and clearly about your audience — about the abilities, needs, interests, pressures, anxieties, enthusiasms, even physical attributes *each one* will bring with him/her to the interaction.

No doubt there will be times when you are not able to get a very clear specification of who will be listening to you. Then you will have to rely on probabilities and/or stereotypes. But there is always danger in using 'typical' specifications for an audience. Go to the greatest lengths that time and protocol will allow to find out who will be interacting with you as you talk.

Perhaps you feel that the wording '... who will be interacting with you ...' is a rather grandiose way of expressing what will happen when you talk to your audience. I cannot stress too strongly the need to see the presentation as an interaction: you are not just doing something to or for a passive audience. Too many speakers treat presentations as displays in the presence of spectators, or as activities similar to house-painting — the objective is to apply information smoothly and evenly! Try to develop a sense of sharing, involving, moving together with your audience. Though they may be silent, they are responding. Never is *nothing* happening. To plan successful presentations, speakers must try to project themselves into the frames of reference of their audiences, and choose what to say and how to say it in the light of how it will look from those frames of reference.

Here is a check-list of questions that must usually be answered:

Audience 'mix'

- Who will be in the audience?

Expertise

- Will the members of the audience all have the same background, qualifications, expertise, and experience in my subject?

- What will be the audience's levels of expertise (what is the minimum knowledge I can take for granted)?

- Will it be necessary to explain to the very expert members of the audience that there are less expert people among them, who have a need and/or right to know what otherwise might be taken for granted?

- Will it be acceptable to use the jargon of my subject, or shall I have to explain it to uninitiated members of the audience?

- What will be the intellectual calibre of the audience, and therefore what will be an appropriate unloading rate, complexity of argument, form of language, length of presentation?

Interests

- Will the audience all have the same needs, interests and expectations?

- What will be the audience's motivation to be present, to pay attention?

Attitudes, beliefs and values

- Will the audience's attitude to my subject, my theme, and me be hostile, sceptical, neutral, mildly interested, enthusiastic, ...?

- Will the audience have general attitudes, beliefs, and values that I must take into account?

Atmosphere

- What will be the psychological atmosphere surrounding my talk (the morale in the company I am speaking to, the relationships, alliances and/or tensions between members of the audience)?

Understanding of the situation

- Will my audience be aware of why *I* am speaking at this time, in this place, on this topic? Will I need to explain?

- What will be their expectations, if any, about the normal length, format, and tone of presentations like this?

Not all the questions in this check-list will be relevant to every talk. You will not always be surrounded by people who bristle at any mention of Work Study, by pressures from inter-departmental rivalry, or by anxieties among office workers who have heard they are likely to be made redundant. Let me stress, however, the importance of thinking not only about your audience's technical needs, interests, and expertise, but also about their general attitudes, beliefs, and values. Decisions to adopt a point of view or agree to a line of action are often strongly influenced by attitudes such as 'I always like to have at least two suppliers, if possible', or by beliefs such as 'Japanese goods are always reliable, and good value for money', or by values such as 'I know I would have greater privacy in an office by myself, but I like the friendly, co-operative atmosphere we've established in our open-plan layout'. To counter those influences, especially when you are planning to persuade (or more diplomatically, lead) your audience to a point of view or a decision, you may need to include in your talk information and comments that would not be required by a strictly logical analysis of the facts of the matter.

Analysing the context

The final questions in the list concerned with analysing the audience have begun to shade over into an analysis of context — of the over-all setting, with all its physical, psychological, industrial, social, and political aspects.

Simple matters such as the venue for the talk will often influence what material you can include. The venue may restrict the range of aids available to you, the ease with which you can hold a question-and-answer session within your presentation, or even the length of time it will be reasonable to ask the audience to sit and listen. No doubt some of you have suffered, as I have, in a stifling room, with torture-chamber chairs, and pillars or projectors carefully placed to block your line of vision. No doubt, too, you have been at a talk at which the speaker has put up an aid and said: 'As you can see from this chart ...', but the flip-chart page or the image on the screen has been so small that you could *not* see, and the speaker's failure to adjust his/her choice of aids to the size of the room has caused you to miss part of his/her material.

Ask yourself:

- How much time will be available for the talk? How much time will it be strategically wise to occupy?

- At what time of day will the talk take place? What will be happening, if anything, immediately before and after my talk that might influence my audience's receptivity?

- Where will the talk take place?
  - Size of room?
  - Arrangement of seating?
  - Availability of visual-aid equipment?
  - Size of image possible on screens, size of chalkboards/flipcharts?
  - Placing of screens and equipment, lines of sight for the audience?

In analysing your aim, audience and context, you will have begun to see what you will have to do to help your audience. You will have begun to see the answers to the following questions:

- What will I have to do to catch and hold the attention of *this* particular group in *this* setting?

- What will it be helpful to put into visual form for *this* group?

- Which visual form will be most helpful in *this* setting?

- How much example and analogy will it be essential, desirable, and possible to introduce to help *this audience* comprehend and assimilate the complexities of my new information?

Planning a talk is always a matter of arriving at a compromise between what is essential, what is desirable, and what is possible. I cannot offer you detailed advice on the compromises you should make in selecting and arranging *your* material; but the next chapter outlines some general tactics that are well tried and reliable.

CHAPTER 3

Assembling material for your talk

Creating an outline

So far, I have discussed the analysis of aim, audience, and context as if it is something you have to do before you think about which elements of your topic to include in your presentation. In reality, you will usually have your subject-matter in the back of your mind throughout the analysis stage. You will have some ideas of what it is essential for you to include — of your priorities, and of the particular emphasis you want to give your presentation. Probably, a general line of argument or plan of campaign will begin to take shape. In some cases, the subject-matter itself will have a distinct structure and/or an intrinsic logic that will impose itself on part of your presentation.

Nevertheless, there comes a point at which you have to sit down and choose which bits and pieces of information you are going to use in your talk, and how to arrange those bits and pieces. You reach the outlining stage.

If you are lucky, the main outline of your talk may be 'obvious'. If, for example, your task is to describe a problem with a fibre-spinning machine, and how to correct it, it is probable that the central part of your talk should consist of a description of the problem and of your suggested solution. You have only to decide how to begin and end the presentation. But if your task is to describe the composition of a new drug and its apparent greater effectiveness than other drugs, the sequence of your talk is not so obvious. Should you give greater emphasis to the composition, manufacture and administration of the drug, and then turn to its effects (and side-effects); or should you start with

Chapter 3

what the drug seems to offer the medical community, leaving details of specification and manufacturing until later? There is no 'obvious' answer. As is so often the case, your choice of answer must depend on your audience's interests and your objectives. Your audience may be medical practitioners, or drug manufacturers, or the regulatory authorities for drugs. Your own objective may be to focus on the drug's immediate benefits to the medical profession, or on interesting chemical features of the compound, or on difficulties of quality control during manufacture of the drug. As you can see, it is not the subject under discussion that dictates your tactics: it is the objective of the presentation.

Which structure?

Beware of 'obvious' structures. Especially, beware of one of the commonest tactical errors — losing the attention and sympathy of your audience by launching into detailed descriptions of objects or processes before you make plain *why* you are presenting all that detail.

Usually, excellent intentions lead speakers into this error. 'Surely', they say, 'I must explain to people exactly what it is that I am talking about before they will be able to follow the intricacies of my case for change'. That is reasonable logic, but not good thinking about catching and holding human attention. Busy audiences want to know why they should listen, what's in it for them. To start with a summary of what is to come, emphasising the 'news' in your message, will normally give a much more satisfying answer to the audience's unspoken question: 'Now, what's this all about, and why should I pay attention?'.

An important practical point: don't expect that you will always be able to start planning your material by noting down the precise bits you will use to start your talk. The best material to use at the start is often not apparent until you have constructed the main body of the talk. Indeed, the exact terms of my conclusions, even the conclusions themselves, are often modified as I oblige myself to give precise formulation to ideas, impressions, and arguments that were milling around vigorously but shapelessly in my mind.

Giving focus and stimulating ideas

Try to formulate a short sentence that states clearly the theme or facts you want to put forward. For example: 'That the best answer to problem X is solution Y'; or 'That our financial position in the second quarter indicates that we should take such and such measures in the rest of the financial year'; or 'That software package X has the following features: ....., ..., and ..... .'.

Then, allow your mind to be triggered by any of the key words in your short sentence, and write as fast as you can a series of notes on the flow of ideas that ensues. I recommend a series of *notes*; other people find it easier to pour out on to the paper a rough-and-ready full text. It really does not matter what system you devise for yourself, *provided* that you recognise that this will be only a first draft of what you will present in your final construction.

As far as possible, keep roughly to the outline structure you first thought of, but don't worry if your flow of thought seems to move away from your original plan. Try not to let odd thoughts escape, however out of place they may seem at the time. Make a note of them on the corner of your note-pad. When I have finished my first stages of preparation, I usually have a central pile of notes, which represents the main flow of ideas I want to express; surrounding that main pile are many odd scraps of paper on which I have noted ideas that do not seem to fit in to the main flow, but which I think I may want to add somewhere. It is untidy, but it keeps my mind open to the possibility of finding a more effective sequence and more effective wording than occurred to me at this first drafting stage. Don't worry about exact sequence and logical connection. Don't worry about correct English. Aim at constructing a rough, note-form synopsis — an outline of intent.

One obvious challenge to that advice is: 'What do I do if no flow of ideas ensues?'. If you have been able to write a theme sentence, and are well-informed about the topic, I find it hard to believe that no ideas will flow. Normally, complete blockages occur only when writers have no clear ideas about why they are writing, about what they want to say. And if you have no clear idea about what you want to say, perhaps you should not talk at all! Or at least, you should go and talk to whoever commissioned (commanded?) you to speak, and clarify what objectives he or she had in mind.

You will note that I use a pencil and paper. I am told frequently nowadays that I should use my computer for this preliminary outlining stage. I acknowledge that a word-processor or computer *can* be used to produce an outline of notes, and to collect 'odd' thoughts that do not seem to fit comfortably into the main flow. If you can do that successfully, by all means go ahead. But I find the small screen too constricting. Computer technology has not yet produced a screen that will simulate the top of my five-feet-wide desk, with main sheets of notes in the centre, and fifteen or twenty extra sheets arranged around the main pile. As I put together a presentation (or a written text), I want to be able to see the whole of the main plan, *and* all the other pieces that might be used to adjust the shape of that plan. Shape and pattern are vital to the ease with which an audience can perceive and comprehend information. A computer screen, even with the use of 'windows', encourages us to think and plan in small chunks. I think it is important to be able to re-assess constantly not only the shape of each chunk but also the over-all pattern of the presentation you are constructing.

Re-assess your rough synopsis or rough draft in the light of all your decisions about aim, audience, and context. Then begin to give the rough material a final shape by looking consciously for a good beginning and an effective ending.

CHAPTER 4

Deciding how to start

Building confidence by starting well

To get off to a good start is important both for you and for your audience. It is vital to your confidence and to theirs.

If the first few moments go well, you have a chance to settle into your stride, comfortable that your choice and sequence of information are proving satisfactory, that your voice sounds normal, and that, though you feel a little tense, you have the tension under control. If you stumble and fumble through the opening moments, it is likely that you will become flustered, that you will lose confidence in your plan, and — as your hesitancy, inarticulacy and blushing increase — your discomfiture will quickly become obvious to the audience.

If your first few moments go well, your audience will begin to feel that they are in the presence of a speaker who has both material and self under control. They will not be distracted by your apparent unease; they will be free to concentrate on what you are saying. They will be able to settle back with reasonable confidence that their listening will be worthwhile. If your first few moments go badly, your audience will quickly become embarrassed and alarmed: embarrassed, mainly, on *your* behalf, because you seem to be in difficulties; alarmed, mainly, on their own behalf, because they seem to face the prospect of an unprofitable and embarrassing period of listening.

What is required for a 'good start'

Fortunately, getting off to a good start is not difficult. By a 'good' start, I mean a businesslike, satisfactory, or competent start. Let me say again that I am not writing with the extraordinary in mind: I am concerned with businesslike competence. Let us aim first at competence and reliability: brilliance can come later!

A sound, reliable start requires five things:

- choice of the right information;
- arrangement of that information in an effective sequence;
- thorough thinking through of the wording and tone required;
- REHEARSAL;
- self-control at the time of delivery.

Choice and arrangement are topics for this chapter; expression, rehearsal, and control of nerves will be discussed in Chapters 12 and 13.

The material at the start of a talk must be concerned with aiding motivation, gaining attention, and providing orientation. What are these three abstractions?

motivation: the audience's drive towards a particular goal or activity

attention: the audience's ability to identify and concentrate on an incoming message *orientation*: the audience's sense of where they are now, where they have come from, and where they are going (sometimes literally but more usually metaphorically)

Aiding motivation

A speaker must take account of motivation by asking first: will the listeners be enthusiastic to be present, to listen to me, and to accept what I say? If your audience will be coming to your talk willingly, you probably do not need to make *special* efforts to establish or increase their motivation as you begin. But if you know some of your audience will be reluctant to attend, it will be good policy to build into your opening remarks some material that will alleviate or remove their disgruntlement.

Choice of suitable material will depend on close analysis of why they are or will be disgruntled. Do they lack enthusiasm for you, for your topic, or for the activity of attending lectures? Will they be resentful because their bosses have compelled them to come, and/or because the talk is scheduled for a Friday afternoon, and/or because it looks as if your talk represents yet another effort from your department to interfere in their affairs? Will there be several of these causes of poor or negative motivation around the room?

Generally, the way to reduce disgruntlement and/or disarm hostility is to show quickly that you have something to offer that will be useful and/or interesting and/or profitable for the listeners. Indeed, if you suspect they will be reluctant to attend your talk, and you have a chance to send out an advance notice, show in that notice some *details* of what you will be offering. (Tactics for writing an advance notice are discussed on pages 28-29.)

If possible, show early in your opening remarks how the audience may profit from what you have to say. They may profit by gaining ideas or information, which may simply make their work easier or may bring financial gain. Show this early, and enlarge on it later.

But audiences do not always expect or want immediate profit. They may attend your talk out of curiosity — because of a wish to know what is going on elsewhere, or out of sheer intellectual interest. If that is true of your audience, give early in your opening remarks some information that will appeal to their curiosity.

Occasionally, your audience may be attending your lecture because of uncertainty or anxiety, perhaps about their own and/or the company's future, or perhaps simply about a temporary production or personnel problem in the organisation. If that is true of your audience, allay that anxiety as quickly as possible; or if you are not able to do so, say so early, and explain what you *have* come to do.

Perhaps you feel that many of the talks that are given in your organisation never have such a clear purpose as to allay anxiety or to offer profitable ideas. The meetings at which your talks have to be given are routine gatherings to disseminate information, at which you have to talk simply because it is your turn to describe what you are doing. Your colleagues are there principally because they are expected to be there. There is no special *point* to be made.

If there really is *no* point to be made, there is little you can do to prompt your colleagues to listen eagerly or with particular curiosity. Suppose, for example, that in the past three months you have run four experiments of the same type as the six you ran in the previous quarter, and you have no significant results; even the fact that there are no significant results is not significant. In such circumstances, my advice has to be, first, that you try to get the organisers of such routine presentations to drop their insistence that turn-taking must be automatic, even if there is no real news to pass on; and second, that you ensure that your presentation of your routine information is as brisk, economical and businesslike as possible. Under no circumstances succumb to the temptation to inflate what you have to say by introducing artificial points of debate or portentous tone.

Perhaps, too, you occasionally have to present bad or unpalatable news. How should you start then?

My advice is still to bring out that news openly in summary or outline at the beginning of your talk; show immediately that you recognise that what you have to say will be unpalatable. Outline the bad news; emphasise the reasons for that news. If necessary, acknowledge in advance that there will be both emotional and rational responses to what you have to say. Emphasise the evidence on which decisions rest. Evidence will not necessarily sweeten a pill of bad news, but will normally help people accept that the pill must be swallowed. Of course, all this can be done only briefly; your full case must come later; but an opening summary will usually help motivate your audience to listen, help focus their attention on the key features of what is to come, and help them see what your presentation is intended to achieve.

Catching and holding attention

The dividing line is faint between what should be called motivating tactics and what should be called attention-getting tactics. Some items of information and some opening statements may serve both functions — to encourage the audience to listen to your talk, and to help them identify and concentrate on what you have to say.

It does not matter what label we give the tactics, provided the tactics are there; labels are simply conveniences for discussions in books like this. What matters is that we think carefully about how to produce the effects we want.

For example, consider what tactics would be effective in the following case. Imagine that you are an organisation's safety officer, and you have to make a presentation to a meeting of department heads about a new procedure for use in the event of fire.

You have a problem: most of us pay lip-service to the importance of safety measures, but we are reluctant to give up our time and attention to actually *doing* something about them. How can you motivate your audience to listen? How can you catch and hold their attention?

An opening such as this might work:

My topic today is a new procedure in the event of fire or other alert. As you know, fire at the XYZ plant last month claimed three lives. My colleagues and I believe that those lives might have been saved if this new procedure had been in operation.	*Emphasises the topic's immediacy and value.*
The new procedure is one that is especially suitable for buildings such as the XYZ plant's and yours,	*Links the XYZ plant, and the audience's premises.*

Catching and holding attention 27

which present special difficulties because of their size and their rambling layout. The procedure is not complicated: it will take at most 15 minutes for me to explain. It is not expensive: it would require us to buy only £2,000-worth of equipment, which is a small price compared with a human life. There *would* be some additional responsibilities and training required from all of us; but there would be no requirement for anyone to take on onerous or dangerous special fire-fighting duties; and the training time — perhaps better called 'rehearsal time' — would be about 10 minutes per month. I am going to propose that we recommend to the Board the immediate introduction of this procedure.

Explains why a new procedure is desirable.

Indicates the time to be taken by the presentation.

Emphasises the commitment that would be required from the audience.

Emphasises the decision that is wanted from the audience.

In that opening, the reference to the XYZ plant is introduced to emphasise the topic's immediacy and value. A link is made between the XYZ plant and the audience's premises, by referring to shared features. The particular need for a new procedure — the size and the rambling lay-out of the premises — is focused on. The amount of time required for the explanation is indicated (to forestall the commonly affected cynicism: 'Is this going to go on for long?'). The commitment required from the organisation in general and from each person in particular is outlined at the start, to indicate that what is coming is not threatening or unreasonably demanding. Finally, at the end of the opening, the speaker makes clear what will be wanted from the audience — agreement to make a recommendation to the Board.

Tactics such as these should help your audience realise that there will be something of interest in your talk. The things you choose to say at the start should focus attention on the salient points you want to stress, and/or acknowledge what will be in the minds of your listeners. And as I suggested earlier, if you have control over the circular that goes out to summon people to the meeting, put some of your motivating and attention-getting devices into that circular too:

NOT

Safety Meeting
20th June 1999, Room 146, 1400 hrs

J. Brown, Manager, Safety and Security Department
'New procedure in the event of fire'

PREFER

> Safety Meeting
> 20th June 1999, Room 146, 1400 hrs

> John Brown, Manager of the Safety and Security Department, will propose a new procedure for use in the event of fire. The new procedure is particularly appropriate for large and sprawling plant layouts such as ours. If such a procedure had been in operation at the XYZ plant last month, it might well have prevented the loss of three lives.

Of course, only *you* can judge whether such an opening, expressed in those terms, would succeed in your context. Precise tactics must always be related to what you know about the individuals in the audience — their experience, their attitudes, and their inclinations.

Establishing your credentials

Sometimes, however, you do not know the audience well. If you are a visitor to an organisation, or even just have come from another department, your audience may know your name and title, but not really who you are. They may not be really clear why you are there or why they are there. They will normally accord you basic courtesies at first: but you will need to establish who you are, why you are there, and why *you* are standing before them. You will have to establish your credentials; you will then have to go on to earn their attention and respect.

Chapter 4

Establishing your credentials does not mean bragging about your brilliance: it means simply providing the information that your audience will consider relevant to the situation. However, it is often difficult to prevent your self-introduction sounding self-congratulating or self-promoting. You may be able to escape from that difficulty if the meeting has a chairman/chairwoman who provides an introduction, and/or if your credentials are summarised on the notice of the meeting. But beware of chairmen and chairwomen! Listen carefully to what they say about you. Especially, listen to what *they* say you are going to talk about. My experience is that they will often announce something slightly different from what you have prepared. Always check with them *before* they set the meeting in motion *exactly* what title has been circulated before you came and/or what title they are planning to use in their introductory remarks.

Especially, listen to see if they provide all the information to answer the queries that will be at the back of your listeners' minds. Those queries will be:

- Who is this?
- Where is he/she from?
- What is his/her background (subject expertise, experience)?
- What authority (knowledge, status) has he/she to justify giving this talk?
- What plan (structure, length of time, arrangements for questions) does he/she have in mind?

This does not call for a laboured curriculum vitae: something as economical as possible will do:

> 'My name is Mary Brown. I am a specialist in computer-aided design at the XYZ Company. I'm a physicist by education, but

> I began to specialise in computer-aided design during an eight-year spell at the ABC Company; and in the three years since I joined the XYZ Company, I've been in charge of the VINCI project. As some of you know, VINCI stands for Very Ingenious New Computer Inputs, and since your new flying-machine design needs inputs such as we've been working on, I'm pleased to have half an hour this afternoon to describe to you three of our main developments. They are: .... '

Note that this opening not only includes the speaker's credentials but also uses an attention-getting reference to the audience's needs. It provides orienting references to the time needed and the number of main developments that will be described. The opening is not a long-drawn-out catalogue of personal data. The speaker is soon moving forward into her topic, beginning by emphasising that she will describe three main developments.

Aiding orientation

Telling the audience in outline what to expect is the most important part of orientation. Discernible pattern, shape or framework is a vital element in perception and assimilation of information, whether the mode of transmission is speech or writing. It is therefore helpful if speakers begin not only by explaining their ultimate goals — what purpose(s) they have in speaking and what conclusions or proposals they intend to lead to — but also by making plain what paths they intend to follow, or through what framework they propose to lead their listeners. This need not prohibit speakers using the valuable element of surprise: but surprise should stem mainly from unexpected facts, unexpected connections, unexpected observations, not from the introduction of unexpected topics. Mary

Brown might legitimately surprise her listeners by mentioning unexpected features of the VINCI project, or by turns of phrase that sharpen the impact of her argument; but she should not surprise them by suddenly introducing a fourth development, when she has announced only three.

Should you keep people guessing?

Sometimes, people question the wisdom of revealing the structure of their presentations at the outset. 'Wouldn't it be better to keep the audience guessing, to play on their curiosity?'

Occasionally, that may be so, but usually only when the topic and the occasion call for (or at least allow) the creation of a slightly arch or teasing atmosphere. If you find that, in your planning of your talk, there comes a point at which you feel that you should say to your audience: 'Now, where's all this leading to?', you can be sure that some of your audience will be asking themselves that question before *you* get to saying it, and it is likely that there will be an element of impatience or exasperation in their minds.

Should you begin with a story or assertion?

Sometimes, too, people suggest that, if they build in the sorts of motivating, attention-getting, and orienting tactics I have been advocating, they will not be able to use special attention-getting devices like illustrative stories or striking assertions. That is not necessarily so. It can indeed be very effective to begin a talk with an anecdote or an intriguing assertion; but there are four important provisos to hold in mind:

- the anecdote or assertion must have direct relevance to the theme and subject of your talk; simply to tell a funny story to help your audience settle into their seats is rarely appropriate in a professional presentation; indeed, they may be so busy enjoying the joke that they miss the moment at which the serious information begins to arrive;

- you must be sure that your humorous anecdote will be funny *to the audience*; there is nothing worse than an attempt at humour that has no-one laughing but the speaker;

- you must be sure that your intriguing assertion can be supported by later evidence and argument; and you must reflect on whether the assertion may seem so preposterous to some of your audience as to be counter-productive — to cause them to reject/resent/resist anything else you say for a while at least;

- your anecdote/assertion must be succinct, crisply encapsulating a point; and the point should be an element that you can incorporate in your orientation segment, which should follow soon after the anecdote/assertion.

Ten attention-getting devices

Many attention-getting devices can be combined effectively with

Chapter 4

the self-introduction and orientation tactics I have mentioned. Here is a list of ten. The list is not by any means exhaustive, and is not in any order of priority or preference. I offer it simply to provoke thought about the best way to get your presentation off to a good start.

- Summarising features/qualities/benefits

  The ABC Instrument measures to x mm accuracy, weighs only y ounces, has only z moving parts, yet ...

- Referring to a common problem

  Every writer or editor knows how easy it is to miss 'typos' or duplication of words like *the*. Proof-reading is a time-consuming and difficult task. At last, a reliable aid has come on the market: ...

- Citing an interesting example

  In the ABC Company, use of Y instead of X has increased output by ...

- Making a startling statement
  (A 'Did you know ...?')

  Such and such an error/oversight can cost a large Technical Publications Department x dollars during a year ...

- Announcing a novelty, comparing new with old

  X, the latest ... package, on the market only since last July, has already taken more than half the market share of the well-known Y, because it has this and that property, and offers ... for the future.

- Referring to an authority

    At a symposium at MIT recently, Professor X stated that ...

- Citing a quotation

    True ease in writing comes from art, not chance,
    As those move easiest who have learned to dance.
    Alexander Pope
    An Essay on Criticism

- Telling about personal experience

    For three years now, I have been using an ABC, made from x, y, and z. At first, I could not ..., but after about four weeks, I ...

- Telling an illustrative anecdote

    About x years ago, a physicist working in ... [anecdote] ... . Since that time, changes in X and Y have ... . Now we can ...

- Presenting a question, to arouse curiosity

    Shall we ever be able to produce X from Y?

How NOT to start

Let me end this discussion of what to say at the start of your talk by recommending things NOT to say.

Never start with self-deprecation. For example, avoid: 'Ladies and gentlemen, I'm afraid I'm not much of a speaker'. If that is indeed true, leave it as long as possible before they find out!

More seriously, my aim is to get you out of the frame of mind that believes you are not much good. The fact that you are reading this book shows that you want to improve. One important step is to begin to think positively about yourself and the task of speaking. So, no professions of weakness, please: turn your thoughts towards delivering competently the businesslike presentation you have constructed.

Similarly, avoid: 'I hope I won't bore you for the next hour'. Your audience hopes so, too! If there is a chance that you will, perhaps your talk needs to be re-planned. And avoid: 'I haven't really anything to say on this topic'. If that is the case, your audience may reasonably wonder why are you up there speaking!

CHAPTER 5

Organising the middle of your presentation

Deciding proportions of time

Perhaps the word 'middle' in this chapter-heading is misleading. We have now to consider how to arrange the main body of your talk, which stretches from the end of the beginning to the beginning of the ending. It is the middle, in that it is between your carefully constructed opening and ending; but in length and content it occupies, as a rough generalisation, about 80% of your time, so it is a wide 'middle'.

Is 80% an exact figure? Certainly not. Your allocations of time may vary in accordance with the task in hand. But audiences have a sense of what is about right for beginnings and endings. Too much time spent on preliminaries, scene-setting, filling in the background, will usually irritate an audience. Equally, if you apparently arrive at your concluding remarks, and then they seem to go on rather a long time, your audience is likely to be disconcerted.

The proportions of time you should allocate to the beginning, the middle, and the end must obviously be chosen in the light of your decisions about the aim(s), audience, and context for your talk. It may help if you think of about 10% of your time for getting started, about 80% for the main discourse, and about 10% for your closing remarks. But these are only rough guides. In a short talk (say, 10–15 minutes), necessary preliminaries may occupy up to 2 minutes (13–20%), and you may need as much as 2 minutes for bringing the presentation to a firm resolution. In a one-hour talk, you should usually be getting down to business by about 4–5 minutes (less than 10%), and your closing stages should not normally exceed that length of time.

I have emphasised that these cannot be exact figures: beginnings and endings may well be longer than I have just suggested. However, I want to emphasise, too, that you should think of minima as well as maxima for your starting and finishing sections. Do not start or finish too abruptly.

At the beginning of a talk, an audience needs a little time to settle down, to 'tune in' to the subject and to you as the presenter. It is a mistake to plunge too rapidly into detailed argument. Also, at the end of the talk, audiences like to be able to sense that you are bringing the presentation to a close. An abrupt finish leaves a sense of surprise, of incompleteness — 'Is that it, then?'. So it is desirable to construct a finish consciously. Tactics for doing so will be discussed in Chapter 6.

Possible ways of organising the main body

It would be convenient if I could give just one set of rules as *the* way to organise the body of a talk. Unfortunately, there are innumerable ways of telling a story or arguing a case. The most suitable structure depends on the aim(s) of the presentation. Since there may be many aims, I can make only a series of generalisations here, which must be adapted in the light of your precise circumstances.

First, some general principles of good communication, whether you are speaking or writing:

Possible ways of organising the main body

- always move from outline to detail;
- always move from general to particular;
- always relate new (unknown) to established (known);
- supply example and analogy to aid assimilation of theory;
- support assertions with evidence, and opinions with reasons.

Beyond these principles, what structures are possible? To set you thinking, here are ten:

- describe a phenomenon, speculate on its cause, describe its effects;

- describe a problem, outline possible solutions, choose one solution and recommend it;

- describe a phenomenon/entity/activity, discuss its variations in particular places/circumstances/relationships;

- give a chronological account of a sequence of events/ activities;

- describe a procedure by design stages/production phases/experimental steps;

- describe the features/qualities/properties of an object/process/idea in order of importance, either in ascending order of importance or in descending order of importance;

- describe varying objects/ideas/processes, compare and contrast them, evaluate them, recommend one or more for a particular purpose;

- describe what is wanted from an object or process, or in a situation, state what is possible, suggest how the shortfall might be made up;

- state a belief, offer supporting reasons;

- pose a question, suggest various answers, propose one as the best answer.

No doubt some of your speaking tasks will call for arrangements or structures other than these. I have listed ten here to encourage you to consider various ways in which you might approach a single task. There is rarely only one 'obvious' way of structuring your information.

For example, imagine that you want to argue for the use of drug A in treatment of a particular condition. There are three other drugs available, X, Y and Z. Drug X is the drug most used for treatments at present. Your audience is generally familiar with the disadvantages and advantages of all the drugs.

You might consider it 'obvious' that you should start with a description of the condition, go on to describe the effects of each drug, list and consider the advantages and disadvantages of each drug, and then state why you think the audience should join you in preferring drug A. This is a common (and rather heavy-footed) way of making comparative or persuasive presentations. (If you are not accustomed to thinking about pharmaceutical topics, you could substitute for this example a parallel case in which you had to propose software package A for a particular application, or building material A for a specific construction.) But other strategies would be possible and, since they would probably reduce the amount of description of what the audience already knows, might be more effective. Here are three:

- start with a condemnation of the effects of drug X, suggest that drugs Y and Z would be no better, then point out why you think that A would be preferable (you might give little or no time to a description of the condition);

- start by praising the achievements of drugs X, Y and Z, then explain why you think the use of drug A would achieve as much or more, especially explaining why you think drug A's disadvantages are less significant than the disadvantages of the other drugs;

- start with a question: 'Why is none of these drugs entirely satisfactory as a treatment for the condition?', evaluate the shortcomings of each drug, then say why you think drug A would be the best to use.

No doubt as you considered those suggestions, you were thinking about how the audience would react to each of the strategies, and were thinking 'Yes, that might be possible' or 'No, that would produce quite the wrong response'. That is precisely the sort of thinking necessary as you produce your strategy for each speaking task.

A strategy for describing and explaining

However, though I have said there is rarely only one way of structuring your information, here is an outline structure or strategy for the most common types of presentations — for reports (on tests, experiments, surveys), for requests (for capital, decisions), for information-giving talks, and for recommendations of solutions to problems:

OPEN

(If necessary:
- introduce yourself
- state your understanding of the task/situation
- state your understanding of the time available)

State your intention and/or objective and precise topic

Outline what will be involved
- make clear the structure of your presentation

Summarise especially:
- what you conclude and or recommend
- what you are offering
- what you want

SET THE SCENE (IF NECESSARY)

? Explain constraints
? Give definitions
? Give background knowledge

NARRATE, DESCRIBE, EXPLAIN, ARGUE .....

Describe and explain objects, processes, ideas
Describe and explain activities, events
Describe and explain outcomes, problems
Present facts, opinions
Balance, relate, discuss implication
Emphasise pattern(s) in your information/ideas

DRAW INFERENCES AND CONCLUSIONS
(IF APPROPRIATE)

FORMULATE RECOMMENDATIONS/
REQUESTS (IF APPROPRIATE)

SUM UP

Leave a clear impression of:
- what has been said
- what is wanted now
- (if appropriate) what will happen next

The 'unloading rate' for your information

When you have made a rough arrangement of your information, pause and reflect whether the information load represented by your chosen material will be acceptable to your audience in the time and circumstances for your talk. Too many speakers ignore their audience's capacities, and pour out their material either too rapidly or too slowly.

The audience will be influenced by two aspects of your 'unloading rate': the density and or amount of information, and your speed of delivery. Reflect on whether your plan is likely to pour out facts and figures too thick and fast. Reflect on the complexity and subtlety of the argument you plan to ask your audience to follow. Reflect on the level and extent of abstraction in your presentation. Remember particularly that *you* have heard all this material before: your audience have not. If the unloading rate needs to be reduced, you may have to leave out some details, or simply to loosen the density or abstraction by introducing helpful examples, analogies or illustrations. It may be helpful to introduce deliberate reiteration and cumulative summaries. And it may even be necessary to plan to slow your rate of speech deliberately at specific points.

Remember that the unloading rate you plan to use will affect you, too. It will affect not only your audience's ability to receive and absorb but also your own ability to handle the information. The more complex the argument you plan to present, the more thorough must be your command over it. At the start of your talk, when you are trying to keep things as easy and flowing as possible in order to establish your own and your audience's confidence, it is especially important that you do not try to launch into a complex argument that ends up in a tangle.

Short-term and long-term memory

In considering unloading rate, you must take into account the demands you are likely to make on your audience's memories. This requires you to recognise which aspects of memory the audience will have to bring into play. Receiving, evaluating, storing, remembering (and forgetting), linking — these are the activities of memory required of a listener while a talk is in progress. They involve both short-term and long-term memory.

Short-term memory is the activity of memory by which we 'hold ideas in mind' while we listen. We perceive what a speaker is saying, comprehend the meaning of the words, evaluate the statements offered, sift the information contained, relate it to past experience, link it with previous elements in the presentation — generally 'reflect' on what is being said. Long-term memory is the activity of recall. It is not just a matter of holding things in mind during reflection: it is the activity of storing and later retrieving, bringing back into circulation information that had been put out of immediate use for a time.

A speaker must give some thought to what the audience will be required to do during the presentation. Will they simply need to reflect on the material while the talk is going on, and have no need to select and store significant facts or ideas; or will they have not only to 'sit and listen' but also to attempt to select, catch, hold, store, and subsequently retrieve significant and substantial parts of the information that is being presented?

If their listening will require mainly short-term memory, you will have to focus primarily on unloading at a rate that will be immediately manageable. If their listening will require memorising of information for the long term, it will be incumbent on you to give them help with recognising the essential information, fixing key words and images in mind, relating the new information to what is already in store, and subsequently retrieving the information for use. This will require you to plan deliberately to point out essential items of information; to introduce, highlight and reiterate key words and images; to allow time for assimilation, and to give examples to aid consolidation; to aid the imprinting of pattern by enumeration and/or listing; even, perhaps, to direct the audience's note-taking. Though we are here verging on aspects of presentation technique (or delivery), it is important to mention these aspects, for they must all be part of your planning, selecting, and arranging activities.

Use of visual aids

You must also recognise that a consideration of visual aids is part of the selection and arrangement process. The inclusion of a point in your argument or some details in your data may depend on the visual aids that will be available. Will you be able to design suitable visual material to present your material clearly? Will you be able to handle the aids competently? Also, use of some forms of visual aids consumes time (for example, use of a chalkboard or whiteboard). That may be useful to you, because the time you take in writing on a board may give your readers a chance to make notes, or simply to reflect and consolidate; but it may be a disadvantage if time is short, and you may therefore feel obliged to change part of your plan to avoid needing to use a board. A discussion of the advantages and disadvantages of various types of visual aids follows in Chapter 9.

CHAPTER 6

Bringing the talk to a conclusion

The term 'conclusion' has two meanings. One is its more specialised, logical meaning: a conclusion is a state, opinion or result arrived at after consideration of evidence (premises) and use of due processes of argument. The other is its more general meaning: a conclusion is an ending, a point at which events are stopped, a last or final activity (without any prior logical operations, connections, or direction necessarily implied).

In planning our talks, we may have to consider one or both meanings. A logical conclusion may not be needed; a 'bringing things to an end' conclusion always will.

Talks do not always contain a logical argument that leads to the drawing of inferences and the assertion of a logical conclusion; but talks should always have a sense of progression, of 'leading somewhere', and audiences are more satisfied if there is a distinct sense of completion or closure. The completion should be suitable from the point of view of the information presented and from the point of view of the relationship established with the audience. In the same way as it is important to begin a presentation with clear signals of what is to come, it is important to construct a clear ending to the discourse or, if you are going to move into a question-and-answer session, the end of a distinct segment of the interaction.

In general, your aim in your conclusion should be to crystallise, summarise, pull together points of view, and emphasise the final position you have arrived at. Apart from that, the following generalisations are possible:

- the topic and goal you announced at the beginning of the talk should usually figure prominently in the closing stages;

- it is often helpful to summarise by referring back to the framework you announced at the outset: 'I said at the beginning that I would ...';

- in your talk, you may have raised several questions, framed various possible proposals, or offered several alternative objects/processes/ideas; you need not always answer all questions, come down in favour of one proposal, or advocate one of your objects/processes/ideas: but you must always leave your audience clear about what you *have* done, and what still remains to be done;

- emphasis should be on conclusions, proposals, what is planned next; in particular, persuasive talks should usually end with a clear statement of what you want from your audience;

- tone should remain firm and confident: use 'In this talk, I have explained ...', not 'In this talk, I have tried to explain ...'; use 'I have put before you this afternoon ...', not 'I hope I have put before you this afternoon ...';

- NEVER end with self-deprecation: 'I'm afraid this has been a rather long and boring account ...'; 'You've been very patient in putting up with me for ...'.

Bringing the talk to a conclusion 49

Your structural signals — the summarising, focusing and reiteration — should normally be enough to show the audience that you are preparing to close the lines of communication, or at least to end the expository part of the interaction. Courtesies at the end may be needed, especially if you are a visitor; but they should be kept brief so that they do not detract from the impact of the message you have left in your listeners' minds.

CHAPTER 7

Preparing your notes

Need for notes

Notes serve two main purposes:

- they ensure that you have organised your material and imposed *some* pattern on it;
- they reassure you, reduce your fear that you will 'dry up' (that is, not know what to say next).

Of course, if you have prepared carefully, you will have imposed pattern on your material before the note-making stage. But if you've been pressed for time, or simply been casual about preparing for your talk, the process of preparing notes will force you to think at least briefly about what you will do in your presentation.

Does everyone need notes? There are a few speakers — those who have natural flair, good memories, sound knowledge of their subjects, and extensive experience of speaking — who do not need notes in front of them. They have the ability to remember a full plan — to remember what to say, when to introduce their visual aids, and how to express their material.

But notice that I refer to their ability to remember their *plans*. In my experience, speakers who *seem* to be able to manage effortlessly without notes have usually put a great deal of effort into planning and thinking through what to say. They rarely extemporise.

It always worries me when I hear intending speakers say 'I don't need to make notes: I can talk about that subject off the top of my head'. Very few of us can extemporise successfully. Normally, when we do, we keep going for our allotted time, but the talk that comes out is a shapeless ramble round a topic rather than a constructed presentation. No doubt, like me, you have been to talks where you have been agreeably entertained by a rambling speaker; perhaps it was one who mused gently, or one who harangued you enthusiastically about a theme; but when you have looked back on the talk, you have been able to recall that the talk was interesting, but you have found it difficult to recall any pattern of ideas — what the speaker really seemed to be driving at. That talk probably was less successful than the speaker thought.

If you use the 'off the top of my head' approach, you may remember during your talk all the points that are important on your subject; but your audience will not take kindly to frequent back-tracking and re-routing: 'Oh, I meant to say earlier that ...' or 'Ah, I should have told you before just how we came to be ...'. Frequent uses of 'Finally, ...' or 'Oh yes, and ...' are irritating signs of inadequate preparation — signs, in my view, of discourtesy to your audience, of the fact that you have not bothered to find the time to prepare to occupy *their* time and attention.

Certainly, if you have given a presentation many times before, and *if* the audience and context that you are to meet are closely similar to others you have met before, your need for analysis and preparation will be much reduced. But even in these circumstances, I would recommend the discipline and security of notes. You may not need to use them much during your presentation, but they will be there to fall back on if you are distracted in some way and lose your track. My own experience as a speaker has been that familiarity very easily breeds oversight, and I now oblige myself to use notes even though I have spoken on a topic many times previously.

Using your aids as notes

Do you need notes if you are using visual aids? Can't the aids serve as your notes?

Obviously, your visual aids will serve as a reminder of what you have planned to say. But there are six points I should like to make here against using your aids as your notes (further discussion of use of aids follows in Chapters 9, 10 and 11):

- you will need to have notes anyway, of when and where to introduce your visual aids;

- your visual aids should be aids to your audience, introduced *from time to time* to help them assimilate what you have to present;

- the temptation, if you use your visual aids as notes, is to have aids on display throughout your talk, more as a prop to yourself than as an aid to the audience;

- it is tempting, if you want to use your visual aids as notes, to write them as notes — to produce images consisting largely of words, which are generally the least effective *visual* aids;

- it is tempting to put too much on each visual image — to crowd several points on a 35mm slide, an overhead transparency, a flip-chart sheet, or other form of aid; this makes the image like a page of notes that you then stand and talk about; as a generalisation, good visual aids will each support *a* point, not several; each aid should go up for a limited purpose, to serve as a focus, on which you enlarge, guided by your notes; you should not find yourself gazing at the aid wondering what else you were going to say about it;

- if your aids are 35mm slides in a carousel, if you have a pile of overhead transparencies, or if you have a set of flip-chart pages clipped in a prepared sequence, it will be very difficult for you to change your plan during your talk if the need arises; if someone interrupts with a question, or if you can see in your audience's eyes that you need to adjust your plan, it is hard enough to shuffle your *notes* to allow yourself to change your sequence: it is well-nigh impossible to shuffle your slides, transparencies or flip-charts.

Your visual aids must be designed principally for the visual impact they will have on the audience. If you can use them also as aids to your memory, that is a bonus; however, I believe you need to be an experienced speaker to do that successfully; so in the early days of your speaking career, play safe and have notes.

My policy in training speakers is to urge them to minimise possible sources of anxiety, to minimise the chances of being surprised and disconcerted. Most beginners are anxious, above all, about forgetting what they meant to say. Notes cannot ensure that you will remember every word that came into your mind during your preparatory 'thinking through'; but they can reassure you that, if you can think of no more to say on your current point, you have a reminder in front of you both of what the next point is to be, and of roughly how you planned to make that point.

How to prepare notes

Your notes will have begun to make themselves during your preparation. That preparation will have left you with a rough synopsis, and your assembled material in unedited prose or outline notes. I should like to be able to tell you that my assembled material consists of neatly annotated 5 x 3 inch file cards, with various colours reflecting the various sections of my talk, and with specially inserted cards to identify my choices of visual aids. But my draft material usually consists of many sheets of paper, of various sizes, with writing in various directions, with bits stapled over other bits, and copious use of 'See Note A' or 'Go to insert C' or 'Insert chunk from back of draft page 6'. That draft material has to be converted into orderly, clear, unambiguous notes for comfortable, unobtrusive use in the talk itself.

Why not use a full script?

Note that I am emphasising *notes*. Let's confront straight away the inevitable question: 'Wouldn't it be a good idea to write the talk out *completely*? That way, you'd be sure to remember everything, and to find just the words you want to express yourself.'

It is undeniable that you would remember everything, and be sure to find your words: but the event in which you would be involved would be a reading in the presence of an audience, instead of an *interaction* in which you *talked to* the audience.

Probably, your reading would be halting and stumbling: few of us are good at reading aloud. One reason for this is that written English is not the same as spoken English. In spoken English, we often use incomplete structures and turns of phrase that would not seem acceptable in written English. Written English is usually more formal. When you read aloud an expression such as: 'It can be asserted with some confidence, therefore, that ...' or 'As has been demonstrated by the above sections, ...', it rapidly becomes clear that you are speaking writing at the audience, not talking to them.

In any case, the audience can *see* that you are speaking writing at them, because as you read, inevitably you lose eye contact with them. Eye contact between audience and speaker is essential to a shared sense of interaction and involvement (more on this topic in Chapter 13). If your eyes meet theirs only in occasional upward flicks, gradually they get a sense simply of watching you reading instead of interacting with you while you speak. And all too often, when speakers do read a script, their upward glances become very infrequent, and are reduced to general upward movements of the head and eyes, without genuine focus on any members of the audience. Then the impression created is of a wish to avoid the audience, almost of furtiveness.

As your head and eyes go down to read your script, it becomes harder for you to speak with clarity and with variety of intonation. Full use of breath and voice calls for you to stand up straight, with head held up to give free play to diaphragm, lungs and voice box. I am not saying that you must adopt an artificial, declamatory stance: simply that you must keep your windpipe and vocal chords as unpressurised as possible.

Perhaps the greatest danger of relying on a script is that it tempts you to be satisfied with less thorough preparation and rehearsal than you *should* demand of yourself. It is tempting to think: 'Well, it's all there. All I've got to do is read it.'. Maybe you *will* read it through a few times in advance of the talk; but will you bother to make sure you are *thoroughly* familiar with your whole scheme? Will you make certain that you really are sure of where in your plan all words and content are scheduled to appear? No doubt you have seen, as I frequently have, speakers turn over a page of their script and look with apparent incredulity at what is written at the top of the next page. They look back rapidly at the bottom of the page they have just finished, and then often to the top of the next page but one, to see if they have mixed up the pages; and then they go on in a tone of strained anxiety, obviously hoping that they will pick up the gist of things again in a moment.

Of course, something similar *can* happen in your use of notes; but in my experience, that is much less frequent. I suspect the reason is that, if you have a script, your preparation focuses on whether you are confident you can *read what you have written on the paper*: if you have notes, your preparation must focus more thoroughly on making yourself confident that you can *recall what you planned to say*.

One final point against having a fully written script: it would be more efficient to give copies to the audience to read. Silent reading is much faster than reading aloud, so distribution of a full text would be a more time-efficient way of transferring your information to your audience.

If you are an anxious beginner, distributing a paper may not sound such a bad idea! But though your message would be distributed in careful wording to all the audience, you would lose the benefits derived from a person-to-person(s) interaction. *You* would lose the chance to see how your message was going over, the chance to adjust your tactics in accordance with the *immediate* feedback from their eyes and general demeanour. *Your audience* would be able to read your words; but they would be deprived of the sense of your worth, your conviction, your knowledge — of the sort of person you seem to be — that they could gain from hearing and seeing you. Whether we like it or not, one reason why people ask us to give presentations is that they want not only to hear what we have to say but also to size us up. It is well worthwhile, therefore, to develop competence at presenting not only our material but also ourselves to the best advantage.

'Thinking through'

The note-making skill to work towards is the ability to sit and 'think through' *in detail* what you plan to say and how you plan to say it, and to make notes of key words and phrases, facts and figures, connections and transitions. I know that some people, especially those who do not have to speak frequently, do not find this easy. They prefer to write out a full text, because that is the only way they can force themselves to think their statement right through; they then disassemble that text into a pattern of notes. That strikes me as unnecessary labour; but we are not all comfortable working in the same way; what matters is the end result; so if you produce notes most efficiently in that way, by all means do so.

Reminders about visual aids

Aim at producing a carefully-thought-through array of reminders not only of your subject-matter but also of your plans for using visual aids. Your notes should be not only a compendium of things to say but also an instruction sheet, telling yourself exactly what to do, when, and how. They should ensure that there will be no point at which you are uncertain what to do next!

On my notes, I leave a wide left-hand margin. In that margin, I put clear instructions. A sequence down that margin might read:

> Switch on OHP (overhead projector)
> Put on transparency 1
> Take off transp. 1, leave OHP on
> Put on transp. 2
> Take off transp. 2, put on transp. 3
> Take off transp. 3, switch off OHP
> Show flipchart 1, then cover
> Show flipchart 2, then cover
> B/B (blackboard) notes
> OHP on, put on transp. 4
> Take off transp. 4, switch off OHP

As I shall discuss further in Chapter 10, it is undesirable to leave visual aids showing after they have served their purpose in the talk. It is undesirable either to keep switching on and off the overhead projector every few seconds or to leave it switched on for long periods without a transparency in place. It is therefore necessary not only to remind yourself when to introduce your visual aids but also to help yourself remember your plans for handling the equipment. Your 'thinking through' must give due attention to the mechanics of handling your aids, so that you can avoid the risk of fluster being caused by uncertainty.

Indications of time

You may find it helpful, too, to put indications of time in your notes. That is, you indicate that you should be at point X by about 10 minutes, at point Y by about 20 minutes, and point Z by about 25 minutes. This is especially helpful if you are interrupted by a question or if you add material at one or more points because you can see your message is not being well received. Your time-indicators remind you that you still have, say, fifteen minutes of material ahead. That enables you to make a decision either to run slightly over your planned time, or to leave out items in the fifteen minutes that lie ahead.

There is a practical problem in this inclusion of time-indicators. If you put in times related to the planned length of your talk (10 mins, 15 mins, 20 mins ...), you have to indulge in mental arithmetic to work out how far you are from the time at which you started. (And if you forget to note the time at the start, the scheme is wrecked!) If you prepare your notes with time-indicators related to your *scheduled* starting-time, your plans are thrown awry (or at least, you have to make some awkward adjustments) if your talk does not begin on schedule.

My choice is to use indicators related to the length of my talk. Long experience has taught me that organisers of meetings are rarely likely to be absolutely punctual in opening their proceedings. A scheduled start at 1400 can frequently mean you get up to speak at 1437, which may well be later than the times you have recorded in your notes for a 30-minute talk!

Being prepared to adjust your plan

While I am discussing problems created for speakers by the organisation, or lack of organisation, of events at which they have to speak, let me add two more pieces of practical advice related to the planning and preparation of talks: always plan to fill slightly less

Being prepared to adjust your plan 61

than the time you are told will be available, especially if you will be introduced by a host or chairman; and always give at least *some* thought to what might be left out — how you should re-shape your talk — if you run short of time.

Even minimum courtesies from an introducer occupy a minute or two; long-winded hosts take up ages. Unfortunately, though audiences may sympathise with you as they suffer at the start, they have forgotten by the end of the talk that *you* were not responsible for the loss of time. As the hands of the clock creep towards time for coffee or for their next meeting, their restlessness is likely to increase.

This does not mean that you must always make savage cuts in your material; it has four main implications:

- if possible, you should find out in advance *exactly* when your talk will take place, and you should think whether you will be likely to be running up against an established time-boundary like lunch-time or going-home time;

- if possible, you should establish what the format of the proceedings will be — whether or not you will be introduced, and how much introduction is likely to be necessary; especially, it is useful to know if you will be one of a series of speakers (if you are, time will inevitably be taken by one speaker clearing up and the next speaker getting ready to begin: will this time be found by arrangement of official breaks, or will the organisation still hope to complete three 20-minute talks within an hour?);

- you should establish very clearly whether the time you have been allocated is supposed to be inclusive or exclusive of a question-and-answer period at the end of your talk;

- you should normally plan to speak for about 95% of the time nominally allotted to you.

I have introduced these practical considerations at this point because I think the right time to take them fully into account is in the construction of your notes. If you have been invited to 'talk for about 30 minutes', you should certainly plan an over-all campaign for about 28-29 minutes. But when you come to the note-making stage, reflect on the possibilities for disruption of your plan. Look at your material, and mentally (or literally) mark chunks that are candidates for omission if for some reason you are short of time. I like to have available a little more material than I am likely to need; so I often have in my notes some chunks of material marked 'if time'. Usually, this 'reserve' material consists of extra examples, illustrative anecdotes, extra details. It will be useful, and will fit comfortably into the talk, if I have time for it; but the talk will have satisfactory coherence and comprehensibility if I have to leave it out.

Sometimes, events run disastrously late. As the final speaker, you are called on to start at the time when the event was supposed to finish. You know that many of your audience are restless, anxious to leave. What then?

Much depends on the precise setting — on your relationship with the whole audience. It may even be possible for you to agree with them that it would be better if you postponed your talk to another occasion. Usually, however, you have to go ahead. In such circumstances, your forethought about what might be omitted will be invaluable. You will be able to present a talk that is not distorted or truncated.

I suggest that you would do well to start with a brief comment on the situation that has arisen — to involve your audience in open recognition of your dilemma. If you seem just to plough ahead, without obvious recognition of the situation, your audience's sense of dissatisfaction may be increased by foreboding, or at least by a feeling that you ought to do *something* considerate of them. Accordingly, a *brief* mention, avoiding any whining tone, of what you were asked to do, and what you now propose, would probably be helpful:

	My remit for this meeting was/	
Ladies and Gentlemen.	Your Chairman asked me/	to talk for
	As you know, my brief was/	

about 30minutes on ..... . Given that we are already at lunch-time, I plan to re-shape the talk into about 20 minutes. I shall do so by omitting ..... [perhaps some illustrative examples or a particular aspect of your topic] ..... . If anyone would like to hear that information, I should be pleased to provide it afterwards.

You will not remove all resentment, and your presentation will inevitably suffer; but you will go some way towards disarming most rational people. You may even *gain* a little goodwill.

Length

How long should notes be? As long as is necessary to make *you* confident. Obviously, it is desirable to keep your notes as short as possible: it is daunting to see a speaker advance bearing a great mass of material; and the longer your notes become, the greater the temptation to make them too full, too close to a full script. There can be no arbitrary measure. I have two comments to offer: one on the relation of length of notes to length of talk, and one on the 'density' or amount of information in your notes.

In proportion to the time available, my notes are usually longer for a short talk than for a long talk. This is because a 10-minute talk requires tighter self-discipline than a 60-minute talk. A plan for a 10-minute talk must be very precise. There is not much room for manoeuvre within a 10-minute span, so it is necessary to work out with great care just what you want to do. Within a 60-minute span, there is room for on-the-spot adjustments and variations of plan, so the notes can leave a little more room for ad-libbing on some points.

As you create your notes, do not be surprised if some sections turn out to be 'denser' or contain more detail than others. For parts of your talk that you know very well, you may need only a few key words or phrases to prompt yourself and keep yourself in control. For particularly complex parts — for example, for complicated proofs or for difficult transitions — you may find it helpful to have more detailed reminders.

Size and layout

Aim to produce notes that are accessible but unobtrusive. It is desirable to keep your notes as small as possible, so that they do not become a distraction to the audience. At the same time, it is essential that you should be able to read your notes comfortably, and accommodate in them comfortably all the reminders you want to include. If you can manage with small cards, they will be valuably unobtrusive. If, however, you feel more comfortable with A4 sheets

Size and layout 65

of paper (210 x 297 mm, 8.3 x 11.7 inches), by all means use them. You will simply have to take care that the size of the cards or sheets does not detract from your presentation.

Above all, make sure that your notes are easy to read. It is amazing how often one sees speakers bending over and peering nonplussed at their notes — even admitting self-consciously 'I can't read my own handwriting'. On the basis of my experience of how many speakers make themselves uncomfortable by being unable to read easily what they have written, let me urge you to:

- write or type in lettering that you can read easily when your notes are on a table or lectern 3-4 feet from your eyes;
- make liberal use of capital letters and/or underlining to highlight key words;
- use colour to help with highlighting and differentiation;
- use indentation to emphasise levels of subordination of your points — to help *you* recognise the shape of your talk;
- use numbers/letters/bullets/dashes to help with enumeration/listing/sequencing.

Use every possible device to make life easy for yourself — to make it easy for you to move into and out of your notes accurately and without hesitation. As you look down into your notes, the reminders must be readily *perceived*: they must be short and incisive enough to go into your eye and mind without a lengthy reading movement. That is why full sentences and paragraphs are not so successful as notes: they take too long to read. And then the reminders must bring back quickly the points you wanted to make, the statements or questions you wanted to frame. They must therefore help you recall quickly and clearly how you planned to express your next point. A note such as:

> Nature of the reaction: like the X reaction
> : high speed – c.30 secs.
> : high temp – c.105C

does not help to remind you that you planned to put this point to the listeners as a rhetorical question:

> Nature of the reaction?: like the X reaction
> : high speed – c.30 secs.
> : high temp – c.105C

or that you planned to emphasise the special features of the reaction:

> Note *special features* of reaction: like the X reaction
> : high speed – c.30 secs.
> : high temp – c.105C

To hold or not to hold?

During your talk, should you hold your notes in your hand or put them on the lectern or table? This is principally a matter related to delivery of the talk; but it does influence the form and content of your notes, so I include it here.

As with the size and length of notes, the general answer to this question is that you should do what makes *you* confident and comfortable. Nevertheless, you must give almost equal importance to the comfort of the audience, and it is true that for the audience, the speaker's notes can be a major distraction.

Notes in your hand are more obviously in view. Your page-turning (or card-turning) is more obvious. You may unconsciously but distractingly flick or ruffle the cards or pages; or, like a dealer, bang the deck of cards or pages on the table to knock them into a neat shape; or, like an origami enthusiast, fold and press the sheets into interesting shapes (with dire results when you want to refer to them again!). You may find yourself waving your notes distractingly at your audience as you gesture, or that your gesturing becomes noticeably one-sided because your gestures have all to be made with one hand. And if you are holding on to your notes, you will find it more difficult to manipulate your visual aids.

However, there are disadvantages to putting your notes on the table or lectern, too. If you have only a table, you may find it harder to read your notes, especially if you are tall. If you put your notes on the table or lectern, you may be tempted to restrict your movement — you may not want to stray too far from your notes. This may mean that you have some awkward moments when you *should* move to work at a blackboard or screen that is some way from the table or lectern. And you will still have to turn your pages or cards: if there is not much room on the table or lectern, there is considerable potential for getting your notes jumbled.

My advice is that you put your notes on the table or lectern for as much of the time as possible. Work out an operating system: arrange a space (in a natural page-turning position on the left, if you can manage it) where you will put your used pages or cards, face down to avoid confusion. (Never write on both sides of a page of notes!) But by all means take your notes with you if you have to move away from the table to talk for a while beside a blackboard or flip-chart. This may be particularly sensible if you have detailed numbers or calculations that you want to be sure to get right. And if you plan to quote verbatim several lines from a book or other source, have the whole quotation written out in your notes. Even have the book ready, with your place clearly marked: there is a small but useful gain in credibility when the audience can see the source as you read it. Then, at the appropriate point, pick up the note or text and read it accurately.

There are practical implications in all this for the form and content of your notes. First, it is important that your notes are on firm, not flimsy, material. This is true even if you plan to leave them on the table: it is especially true if you plan to pick up your notes at any time. Is it *really* necessary to offer 'trivial' advice like this? Yes. I have seen many speakers give themselves unnecessary moments of difficulty by preparing their notes on what seemed like air-mail paper or 'copy' paper for use in typewriters. Similarly, it *ought* not to be necessary to advise people against using voluminous computer-print-out sheets for their notes, but I have seen .....!

Second, your decisions about what to include in your notes must be related to your decisions about how you will present the information concerned. You must think about the total context and activity: what your audience's needs will be at the given point, what you will be saying, what will be on a visual aid, where you will have just come from (in the sense both of discourse and movement), and where you will be going next. And in all this, your over-riding concern, from the note-making point of view, must be to put on your pages or cards reminders and instructions that will enable you to move comfortably through your talk both physically and logically.

CHAPTER 8

Deciding whether to use visual aids

How visual aids help you and your audience

In discussions of visual aids with newcomers to the trade of speaking, I frequently meet two very different points of view. One can be paraphrased like this:

> 'Why should I use visual aids? If this is supposed to be a *talk*, why shouldn't I just talk? Handling visual aids will just be one more thing to worry about.'

The other takes a form such as:

> 'Is it all right if I use visual aids all the time? Visual aids give me a prop to lean on. They take the audience's attention off me a bit.'

My reply is that visual aids usually contribute something substantial to a presentation, but that they should not take over entirely as the centre of attention. A talk is likely to be more dynamic and interesting if the speaker seems to be a person in control, not a person subservient to mechanical devices.

The first, sceptical, view has some justification: the introduction of visual aids *does* give you something extra to think about. But visual aids help both you and your audience in five main ways:

Chapter 8

- dealing with numbers;
- dealing with physical objects and processes;
- dealing with abstractions;
- varying the mode of your presentation;
- reinforcing and consolidating your message.

Help in dealing with numbers

Many professional presentations require the introduction of data such as costs, output figures, or projections for markets. Many also require the use of chemical or mathematical equations in arguments or calculations. The handling of numerical data in speech is difficult for both the speaker and the listener. The provision of a visual image helps the speaker present the numbers without stumbling, and helps the audience to perceive the numbers accurately and to assimilate them comfortably. It is vital to recognise, however, that manipulation and memorising of many numbers puts considerable demands on your audience's short-term memory, even when you use visual aids, and in Chapter 11 (General advice on designing visual material), I emphasise the desirability of keeping the presentation of numbers to a minimum.

Help in dealing with objects or processes

Would it be possible to discuss detailed modifications to a factory layout, or the interwoven paths of a complex production plan *without* visual aids? Perhaps. But your audience almost certainly would be helped if they could both hear and see what you were proposing. Your initial statements about layouts and plans might be comprehensible in words alone: but when you were suggesting modifications, and your listeners had to hold some parts of their mental images constant while adjusting others, they would find it invaluable if *you* provided a visual image for them to focus on and manipulate.

As you reflect on the need for a visual aid in a talk about physical objects or processes, much depends (as always) on how familiar your audience are with the topic/entity/activity you are talking about. It is easy, however, to over-estimate the audience's familiarity. You may be tempted to think: 'They are all thoroughly familiar with our storage-tank layout'. But your audience may not have walked through the area as recently or as often as you have. Their impressions of inter-tank spacing may not be as accurate or as fresh as yours, and their memories of where the hatches are on all seven tanks may be somewhat vague. If you give them all the same visual image to look at, you do your best to remove one of the biggest obstacles to efficient communication — the mistaken assumption of mutual understanding. Provide the aid showing the tank layout; then take a careful decision about how much description and explanation of the aid you will need to add. That decision will probably be more difficult than the decision whether or not to include the aid itself.

Help in dealing with abstractions

The provision of the same visual image for everyone to look at is even more important in the discussion of abstract ideas. The trouble with ideas is that they have to take shape in our minds; in each

72   Chapter 8

listener's mind, the words received have to be converted into a mental image. That creates untold opportunities for variety and confusion!

For example, you may be tempted to suggest that a group of computer routines is 'nested', or that a particular action is 'like opening a Pandora's box', or that a laser beam can be given 'a multi-spot or donut configuration'. Those seem helpful images. But I wonder if my images of a *nest* and of *nesting* are the same as yours. Is the nest *shape* significant? If so, is it a shallow, concave nest, like a blackbird's? Or is it a flat platform like a wood-pigeon's? Or is it an enclosed space with one or two restricted access routes, such as a bluetit might construct? And is your notion of *nesting* one of quiet, undisturbed warmth, or one of vigorous, squabbling efforts to grab food or escape? Are all your readers familiar with the story of evils and afflictions escaping from Pandora's box? And if you liken something to a 'donut', what shape do *you* have in mind (and why are you using American spelling)? Is a standard donut a circle of dough with a hole in the middle, or is it a solid lump of dough with jam in the middle? Note how hard I am having to work to try to make clear the two possible shapes I have in mind!

By all means, use verbal imagery and analogy to help your audience establish in their minds the idea you have in yours; but beware of relying on verbal imagery alone: recognise that it will often be necessary to add a visual image to do all you can to ensure that you and your audience have the same idea in mind.

A caveat: visual images need a verbal frame

But beware, also, of relying on visual images alone. Be sure that

A caveat: visual images need a verbal frame

your visual images are immediately recognisable by all your audience. Be sure that your analogies are not too far-fetched. And be sure to plan carefully the key words that you will use to accompany your visual images.

Usually, it is not good policy to leave your visual images to 'speak for themselves'. Sometimes, no doubt, that will be possible; but in professional presentations, we are rarely able to use visual material that will speak to our audiences with the eloquence of newsreel footage. Usually, audiences are helped by the provision of a verbal framework; the words help the listeners link the new information or ideas with their existing conceptual frameworks.

Pictures focus attention, while what is learned is fixed in our minds by words. Captions on charts and drawings have an important influence on *how much* and *what* is remembered. The 'voice over' plays a vital part in our comprehension of documentary films or television. Naturally, the verbal accompaniment must be chosen with sensitivity, so that it does not seem patronising or banal; but usually a verbal accompaniment is necessary. You should plan carefully the key words and phrases you will use in your captions and in your commentary. You should plan to tell your audience what you want them to see, and how you would like them to handle your ideas and information.

Equally, you should be careful not to put up a list of numbers or a pattern of equations, and then hurry past them without explanation. Will it be enough just to say: 'As you can see, these figures/ equations give ample support to my case'? Probably not. At least, your audience will need time to absorb the implications of the display; probably they will need to be helped by brief and sensitive focusing of their attention on how and why the numbers or equations support your case.

Help in varying the mode of your presentation

The main 'mode' of a professional presentation is usually straightforward oral exposition — you stand and talk to your audience. It is possible to change to a second oral mode — question and answer, either rhetorical or actual. A third mode is a combination of oral and visual presentation by the incorporation of visual aids — you talk about images, tables or charts that you show or hand out to the audience. An extension of this third mode (or a fourth mode if you prefer) is discussion, either with or without a visual aid. The longer your presentation, the greater the need for variation in mode.

Even in a 10-minute presentation, your listeners are likely to feel the need for variation. After four or five minutes of simply listening to exposition from you, your audience will probably find it easier to maintain their attention and focus if you introduce another visual element besides yourself. Much will depend on the density and type of information. It may not be necessary to introduce a visual aid: a change from expository mode to question-and-answer mode may be enough. But often it is helpful if you change the principal object of your audience's visual focus, simply as a means of bringing variety into the presentation.

Note that I speak of 'changing the *principal* object of your audience's visual focus' when you introduce a visual aid. Remember that you *always* have one visual aid — yourself! *You* are the principal focus of your audience's attention when there is no other aid. When you introduce a picture or chart for them to look at, you introduce another point of visual focus. That requires thought: do you then want your audience to move their attention entirely to the aid, or do you want them to move their attention to and fro between the aid and yourself? Both are reasonable aims: but your aim needs to be thought through carefully, because your decision will have implications for whether you introduce an aid, what you decide to put on it, what you plan to say in your accompanying commentary, and where you plan to stand as you progress through the talk.

If you want attention focused fully on the aid, you literally step aside. You direct your audience's attention away from yourself by saying something like: 'Now I'd like you to look at ...'; and you take up an ancillary position beside the board, screen or other equipment you are using. If you then want to draw your audience's attention away from the board or screen while you lead them to reflect on a particular implication, or while you give an example to reinforce what is on the aid, you must plan to move yourself physically back into the centre of attention. You must help the audience shift their attention by offering some guiding words such as: 'Let's leave that illustration for a moment while we consider the implication of ...'.

Help in reinforcing and consolidating your message

Visual aids help speakers to reinforce and consolidate their messages, by helping the audience perceive what is being said, and by helping the audience build a cumulative sense of the over-all discourse.

The need for reinforcement is greater in speech than in writing. If readers of a written document fail to grasp the message when they first read it, they can look back and re-read some or all of what has been said so far. If listeners fail to grasp the message when they first hear it, they cannot look back: their only option is to struggle on, hoping to pick up the threads. It is therefore valuable if speakers make special efforts to:

- help listeners perceive their messages accurately at first delivery, by offering those messages through both sight and sound;
- help listeners remember what has gone before by offering cumulative summaries through both sight and sound.

Visual summaries can be especially helpful, because the shape of the visual image can help impress the pattern of information on the audience's minds.

Should you use visual aids all the time?

So far in this chapter, I have given five strong reasons for including visual aids in a talk. Given those reasons, would it not be desirable to use aids most, if not all, of the time? Rarely.

One serious objection is that the audience's sense of contact with the speaker is reduced. To varying extents, depending on the type of visual-aid equipment used, the speaker recedes to an ancillary position. Also, the audience frequently get the sense that the speaker is being carried along by the visual aids, rather than being in control of them. Changes *can* be handled unobtrusively; but my experience is that they frequently become mechanical: the aid is changed, there is a momentary pause as the speaker peers at it, and then the talk continues.

Another serious objection is the lack of flexibility possible when you have a continuous sequence of visual aids planned to fill every

Should you use visual aids all the time? 77

minute of your time. If, because of your audience's response, you feel you ought to make a change in your scheme, it is less easy to do so if you are relying on a continuous sequence of visual aids to get you from point to point.

A third serious objection is that you may be tempted to lose variety in your presentation by operating in a single mode throughout your talk. This need not happen, because you can introduce variety by varying the type and position of the equipment you use; but I am afraid experience tells us that speakers all too often get fixed beside an overhead projector or a flip-chart, and ignore the monotony that this entails.

A common error made by speakers who use visual aids all the time is that they show aids to 'reinforce' material that really does not need it. Audiences feel patronised when a visual is shown to 'illustrate' a word, phrase or concept that can readily be comprehended without it. For example, for a naval audience, a separate slide showing the two words 'Sonar buoys' accompanying the opening statement 'I'm going to talk to you today about sonar buoys', is a visual insult rather than a visual aid.

Another common fault among speakers who leave visual aids on all the time is that they frequently get their commentary out of synchronisation with their visuals. They finish talking about one visual, and begin talking about their next point. But the next visual is not relevant for a minute or two, so they leave visible the visual that is no longer relevant. That can be distracting or even confusing for the audience. To overcome this difficulty, some speakers choose to show a fresh visual aid even though in their commentary they are not quite ready for it. That again can be distracting or confusing.

So where does this discussion leave us? My summary is this. It is very likely that a professional presentation will benefit from the use of visual aids. It is not possible to specify a fixed rate-per-minute for the introduction of visual material, or even a fixed percentage of your time during which visual aids should be used, because your decision must be dictated by your topic, your aim, your audience, and the context for your talk. A talk to schoolboys, describing the four-stroke cycle of a petrol engine, might require visual material on show for 80-90% of the time: a talk to politicians, trying to persuade them of the need to control emissions from factory chimneys, might require visual material on show for only 10-20% of the time. In general, think very hard before you decide to use one mode of presentation, with or without visual aids, for more than 50% of your time.

CHAPTER 9

Deciding which visual-aid equipment to use

Factors that influence your choice

Given that you have decided to use visual aids, which equipment should you use?

Though manufacturers of overhead projectors and 35mm-slide projectors might like you to think so, the choice is not automatic. For example, if your audience is to be just two or three potential clients, seated round a table in a small office, it would probably be a tactical error to plan to use an overhead projector or a slide projector. The equipment itself would loom too large, both taking up space and creating a barrier between yourself and your audience. You would probably have to project your images on a screen or wall, thereby directing your audience's attention outwards, away from the table: it would probably be preferable to use a means of drawing attention inwards, of focusing on material on the table, fostering a collective sense of involvement, a sense of 'gathering round'. You might be able to do this by using a modern slide-projection unit that looks like a small television set with a carousel of slides on top, but such units are not widely available at present. That equipment also locks you into an established sequence for your talk (it is not easy or desirable to flick to and fro to pick out individual slides); in a small-group presentation, it is usually best to be ready to change your scheme in response to questions and observations, and other forms of visual aids make it easier to do that. Probably, your best choice would be to use handout sheets that you could pass comfortably to your audience as needed. Alternatively, you might use an artist's A3

Chapter 9

drawing pad (297mm x 420mm, about 18 x 12 inches), and hold up that pad for display at appropriate moments.

If you know that you will have to give two (or more) presentations on the same topic during a visit, one to an audience of two or three, and one to a larger group, you should prepare two (or more) sets of materials, to ensure that you produce the best possible effect with each presentation.

Your choice of visual-aid equipment must arise out of consideration of:

- the resources (including time) you have for preparing material for use on the equipment;
- the range of equipment available at the venue for the talk;
- the size of the audience, and the size and layout of the room allocated for the talk;
- the level of formality you wish to establish.

Some circumstances limit your choice. For example, if you have to address a group of 500 people in a large auditorium, you will almost certainly have to use a 35mm-slide projector, because that is the only equipment that will give you an image large enough and sharp enough for everyone to see. You may be lucky enough to be invited to work in a purpose-built auditorium, with large screens linked to varieties of special equipment (slide projectors, overhead projectors, videotape machines); but in more than 30 years as a professional lecturer, I have worked in only three such rooms! In most companies, research centres, government departments and educational institutions, be ready to work with less exotic equipment!

Factors that influence your choice 81

In Chapter 2, I urged you to obtain as much advance information as possible about your audience. At the same time, find out as much as you can about the venue for the talk. If possible, take a careful look at the venue before you begin the final stages of your planning and preparation. If you cannot look at the room yourself, ask for a sketch plan. At least, make a phone call and elicit as many details as possible about the physical and human environments for your presentation.

Remember, when you enquire about the equipment available, to ask not only about projection equipment but also about the size of the screens or wall areas available for projection. Time and again in my lecturing career, I have been given powerful projectors, but only small, portable screens that have sharply constrained the scale and type of image I could plan to project.

Remember, too, to ask not only about the size of the room but also about its layout. Are the boards/screens/flip-chart fittings in fixed positions? Is the speaker's table/lectern in a fixed position? What space will you have for movement between lectern, equipment and board/screen? Will all members of the audience have a clear line of sight to you and to all your aids? Will they be arranged 'theatre style' (in rows) or 'boardroom style' (facing inwards around a rectangular or round table)? Will they have a table or other surface to lean on at their seats?

The answers to these questions will help you establish whether you and your visual aids will be visible, and will help you answer three more questions:

- Should I distribute handouts during my talk (will I be able to move freely to distribute the sheets, and will the sheets get round quickly and comfortably?)?

- Should I integrate a question-and-answer session during my talk (audiences like to be able to see questioners, not to have to crane to see where a question is coming from; and intra-audience discussion is difficult to promote in a theatre-style arrangement)?
- Should I plan to remain at the table/lectern most of the time or to move to the board or screen on which my aid is displayed; should I plan to have a colleague help me with the handling of my visual aids?

You may be thinking that these are great lengths to go to over a small presentation. If it *is* 'small' in scale and importance, of course you can scale down the time and attention you give to the preparation and planning. But my philosophy is that *no* presentation is *un*important. Every time I get up to speak, I want to give a presentation that is coherent, appropriate, competent — that 'goes over' well. On the assumption that you want to do likewise, my advice is that you make every effort to eliminate possibilities of surprise and fluster. As one hotel-chain slogan used to put it: 'The best surprise is no surprise'. Be prepared.

When to create your visual materials

One further general consideration: should you plan to use visual materials that you create on the spot (for example, drawings or calculations on a chalkboard), or should you use materials that you plan and prepare in advance?

The answer to this question depends on the amount of time you have available, and whether it will be especially helpful for your

When to create your visual materials 83

audience to see your visual material built up 'before their eyes'.

The physical process of writing or drawing on a chalkboard, flip-chart, or overhead transparency takes time. It is usually desirable, though not always essential, that you should not talk too much while you are writing. There are three main reasons for this: the first is that you need to think carefully about what you are writing; the second is that you need to ensure that your speech does not become indistinct because you are turned away from your audience; the third is that your audience will be irritated if they cannot see exactly what you are talking about because your writing/drawing hand (or your body) is obscuring what you are producing.

So you must take a conscious decision whether or not to use some of your time in producing your material on the spot, with an inevitable slowing down of the pace of your presentation. Usually, you can reveal a flip-chart or display a transparency rapidly and smoothly, sustaining the impetus of your talk. But slowing the pace of your presentation *may* not be a bad thing. It may be valuable for your audience to see clearly how you create a connecting path from A to Z on a diagram, or to have time to reflect on a method of calculation as they watch you use it. In those circumstances, it may be helpful if you do not use a prepared transparency to present a piece of information, but turn deliberately from the overhead projector to a chalkboard for a certain segment of your talk. Or you may decide on a compromise: to introduce part-prepared pictures, diagrams or calculations, and then to complete them on the spot.

If you do choose to create materials on the spot, plan in advance as much possible of what you will write or draw. No doubt you will sometimes want to leave open until the moment of writing your choice of words or images; but as in so much else to do with effective speaking, preparedness is the key to confidence and comfort: so think through what you will want to say and show, and put reminders in your notes of the precise words, numbers, or outlines you will wish to present. (More on the design of visual materials in Chapter 11.)

Using more than one type of visual-aid equipment

Finally, before we go on to discuss the advantages and disadvantages of the most common types of visual-aid equipment, one general tip: consider using more than one type of aid in your presentation.

Speakers have a habit of fixing on one type of aid — for example, an overhead projector — and using that aid alone throughout a talk. That introduces an element of sameness to the talk, especially if you use many transparencies. You can bring variety to your talk by planning deliberately to use another aid for some of your presentation. For example, it is often useful to plan to use an overhead projector as your main 'working surface', and to use a prepared flip-chart to provide a cumulative summary of what has been covered so far. Of course, two overhead projectors (if such lavish provision is available to you!), two flip-charts or two boards can be used with similar effect.

Advantages and disadvantages of common types of equipment

In the next 38 pages, I discuss the advantages and disadvantages of the most common types of visual-aid equipment:

- chalkboards and white boards pages 85–87
- flip-charts pages 87–88
- overhead projectors pages 89–94
- prepared large-scale sheets pages 94–96
- physical models or samples pages 96–98
- handouts pages 98–112
- 35mm-slide projectors pages 112–116
- filmstrips and films pages 117–118
- videotapes pages 118–120
- closed-circuit television pages 120–121
- audio aids pages 121–122
- multi-media page 122

For the main types of equipment, I offer:

— a general comment;
— a statement of advantages and disadvantages;
— notes on what the type is especially useful for;
— tips on planning to use the equipment.

❑ Chalkboards and whiteboards

Traditional chalkboards and modern whiteboards (on which you write with felt-tip pens of various types) are particularly suitable for small, informal presentations, especially if you want to move gradually from a talk to a discussion. The size of image you can create comfortably prevents you using them in presentations to large groups.

Chapter 9

Advantages

- You can easily rub out parts of a drawing and show the effect of substituting other elements.

- Your audience see precisely how you develop an image or calculation.

- You give your audience time to assimilate information as you write, draw or calculate on the board.

Disadvantages

- The size of the image you can create comfortably is small, which prevents you using boards in presentations to large groups.

- Anything complex requires skill in drawing or handwriting.

- You use up some of your allocation of time as you write, draw or calculate on the board.

- If you have only one board, you may have to remove material that you would have liked to keep available.

Especially useful for:

- putting up key words

- adding 'extra' material outside your main plan (for example, demonstrating how you derived a formula that you had not expected to have to explain)

- cumulative summaries, gradually built by adding succinct and *planned* headings as you progress through your talk.

Tips on planning

1. Plan *precisely* what you will put on the board.

2. Plan to keep wording short, and to keep drawings simple.

3. Plan to keep separate areas of the board: for example, one for cumulative summary, one for key words or numbers, one for general working or drawing.

❑ Flip-charts

Flip-charts are suitable for small-group presentations, either formal or informal. You can prepare flip-chart sheets in advance, or use them as a writing pad in place of a chalkboard or whiteboard. The size of the flip-chart sheets, and therefore of the images you can create, prevents you using them in presentations to large groups.

Advantages

- You can have your chart(s) wholly or partly prepared before the talk, and you can leave some spare sheets available for on-the-spot working.

- You *can* refer back to material that has gone before (though that is a clumsy business, so if you plan to repeat material, have a repeat chart).

Disadvantages

- The small sheets restrict the amount of material you can put on a page, and the size of the lettering you can create limits the use of flip-charts to fairly small presentations.

- The pens are often distractingly squeaky and messy during on-the-spot writing.

Chapter 9

Especially useful for:

- small-group presentations, formal or informal, especially when you are a visiting speaker, and you want to be sure that you have everything under your control when you arrive at the venue for your talk

- putting up or revealing key words

- putting up or revealing definitions, especially if you want to leave them visible while you go on with your talk, using another aid

- gradually revealing a prepared summary as you progress through the stages of your talk.

Tips on planning

1. Plan to have two or more charts when you want to make comparisons.

2. Place the flip-chart comfortably for yourself and your audience *before* you start your talk.

3. Always check the line(s) of sight for *all* your audience before you start your talk, especially if you plan to use a flip-chart in addition to another aid.

❏ Overhead projectors

The overhead projector (OHP) was designed to overcome many of the practical problems inherent in using 'old-fashioned' aids. In theory, it enables you to stay facing your audience while you talk about an image that is projected above your head. You can use it to project images from prepared transparencies, or you can use it as a writing surface, using special pens to write on blank transparent sheets.

In practice, its use brings a range of problems not attached to using other aids. The machine itself is bulky, and unless you are in a room specially designed to accommodate it, the machine itself will probably be in the line of vision between the screen image and some of your audience. You, too, are likely to be an obstacle between your audience and the on-screen image. In theory, the image should be *overhead*, but in most rooms, the image is simply projected *behind* the speaker. Consequently, if you stand beside the machine and write or point on your transparency (as is theoretically desirable to keep you in maximum contact with your audience), you block someone's view of your on-screen information.

The OHP is, however, probably the most useful piece of visual-aid equipment widely available at present, so let us reflect on the advantages and disadvantages that should be weighed in your decision whether or not to use it. (Those of you who are in organisations where everyone seems to use OHPs automatically, note that there *are* some disadvantages to be weighed in the balance.)

Advantages	Disadvantages
❏ An OHP enables you to face the audience — maintaining eye contact — while you talk about an image that is projected above your head, so that you do not block the view of the image for any of your audience.	❏ To get the true benefit of using an OHP, you have to find a room that permits you to project an image above your head.
❏ You can project images from prepared transparencies, thereby saving the time that you would lose if you had to write or draw on the spot.	❏ If all your visual material is in the form of prepared transparencies, it may be difficult to depart from your prepared scheme if need arises.
❏ Prepared transparencies can be of high-quality artwork.	❏ A normal overhead projector accepts limited-size transparencies, usually smaller than an A4 (210mm x 297mm) page. This means that the number of words or the size of the drawing you can put on a transparency is restricted.
❏ You can use the OHP as a writing surface during your talk, using special pens to write on blank transparent sheets.	❏ The machinery itself is frequently noisy; pens often dry up while you are using them; the heat and glare become uncomfortable if you write frequently and for long periods on the OHP plate.

Overhead projectors

Advantages (continued)

- You can use part-prepared transparencies, and fill in the gaps on the spot.

- You can build up composite pictures by laying one transparency on top of another, or preferably by planning a sequence of pictures that gradually show more detail.

- Though it is difficult and undesirable to rummage in your pile of transparencies to find a particular sheet, it *is* possible to make on-the-spot changes to your prepared sequence, if necessary (which is not possible if you are using a 35mm-slide projector).

- You can show outlines of objects by laying them directly on the plate of the projector, and you can emphasise the scale of these objects by putting beside them a familiar object (like a coin or a ruler).

Disadvantages (continued)

- You almost always block the view of your on-screen information for some of your audience some of the time, both with the machine itself and with your own body.

- If you avoid blocking the view (as far as possible) by moving away from the OHP, you have either to take your notes with you, or leave them out of reach on the table/lectern.

- Few lecture rooms are designed with the tilted screens necessary to accept images from OHPs without distortion, which further restricts the area available for writing or drawing on the transparency.

Chapter 9

Advantages (continued)

- Special electronic equipment is available that allows images from a computer to be projected through an overhead projector on to a large screen. The speaker can display virtually any material that exists in the computer's database. The text and images projected through the OHP on to the large screen can be manipulated from the computer's keyboard just as if they were being shown on the computer screen alone. In effect, the presenter has available all the resources of his/her windowing, text-processing, and graphics packages not only for use during preparation of the presentation but also during the presentation itself. (See also multi-media, page 122.)

Disadvantages (continued)

- Most of the special equipment currently available requires partial or complete darkening of the lecture room, which makes speaker:audience contact difficult, has a soporific effect on the audience, and makes note-making almost impossible. The speaker has to concentrate on operating the keyboard accurately, usually from a seated position, which further disturbs speaker:audience contact. And when the room is darkened, and the OHP has been adapted to work with a computer, there is little scope for varying the mode of presentation, or for using two or more aids.

Especially useful for:

- building composite images (by overlaying or preferably by having a sequence of transparencies)

- showing comparative effects of changes (by overlaying)

- demonstrating material from a computer screen to a large audience.

Tips on planning

1. Before you begin to plan your transparencies, try to check what size transparency will be acceptable on the projector you will use. If that is not possible, be conservative — for example, plan to fill slightly less than the whole length of an A4 transparency.

2. Remember that the legibility of what you put on your transparencies is affected greatly by the size of the *image on the screen*. You must plan your transparencies with one eye on how much you can comfortably put on the transparency itself and one eye on the size to which it will be possible to enlarge the image. You may have a powerful projector and a giant screen; but that may mean that you have to stand the projector far off among the audience to take advantage of its focal length. If you want to keep your projector in a manageable position near to your table/lectern, and yet have an easily legible image on the screen, you may have to increase the size of your lettering/drawing, and therefore reduce the information you put on each transparency.

3. As a rough rule of thumb, ordinary typing should be enlarged to at least double its original size to be easily legible to readers 20 feet away.

4. Plan to build rather than reveal. Most audiences are irritated by the teasing effect if you put a transparency on the OHP, cover most of it, and gradually reveal additional items. A more acceptable technique is to *add* material, either by overlaying or —

preferably — by designing a sequence of transparencies, each with a little more information.

5. Ensure that an OHP to be used for transmitting material from a computer has an especially powerful light source.

More advice on handling an OHP is given in Chapter 10, *Handling visual-aid equipment*, pages 123–135.

❑ Prepared large-scale sheets (including printed wall-charts, maps and plans, diagrams, algorithms, photographs)

Printed wall-charts or maps, enlarged photographs, or similar large-scale materials can be extremely effective, especially because they often look professional and have special aesthetic qualities. But they must be large enough for everyone to see clearly; they must be absolutely appropriate to the occasion, with no extraneous content; and they must be easy for you to manipulate. If you are tempted to use them, be quite sure that you:

- have somewhere to hang them or stand them unobtrusively (preferably out of sight) until the point at which you want to use them, and after you have finished with them;

- have somewhere to hang them or stand them so that they are clearly visible to everyone while you use them;

- have the strength and space to manoeuvre them when you want to put them up and take them down.

Be sure, also, that you could not get the same effect more

Prepared large-scale sheets 95

economically and more manageably by using a prepared slide or transparency of the same material.

Advantages

- Photographs, especially, bring an air of realism into your presentation, and professionally produced material can be very clear and aesthetically pleasing.

Disadvantages

- It is tempting to use a printed chart or large photograph because it looks good and is available, even though it is not quite right for the communication task in hand.

- You must have somewhere to hang or stand your materials, preferably out of sight, until you want to use them, and after you have finished with them.

- You must have somewhere to hang or stand your materials so that they are clearly visible to everyone while you use them.

- You must have the strength and space to manoeuvre your materials when you want to put them up and take them down.

- Printed maps usually have far more detail on them than is

Disadvantages (continued)

needed for a talk. Be sure this extra detail will not be distracting.

Tip on planning

NEVER plan to have a single copy of a small drawing or photograph to hand round for the audience to look at. If you *have* only a single copy, plan to hold it up to show that you have it, talk about it as best you can, and then invite your audience to inspect it and handle it at the end of the presentation.

❑ Physical models or samples

Physical models have advantages over other aids only when you need to show three-dimensional qualities. Then, a model may be more efficient than a transparency, a slide, or a drawing. But it is difficult to have models large enough for demonstration to large groups. One way of overcoming this difficulty is to use closed-circuit television or a video film of the model, but that presupposes the availability of the necessary equipment — still rarely available, even in universities, in my experience.

If you decide to use a model, plan to keep it out of sight until it is needed, and to put it away when you have finished with it, so that it is not a distraction at other times.

Samples may occasionally be very helpful; but they must be introduced with care. The more intriguing and interesting the sample, the more distracting it is likely to be. If you give out

Physical models or samples

samples, you must plan to make substantial use of them; that is, you must have a good deal to say about them, so that you guide the audience's examination of them. If you give them out, and then dismiss them abruptly, it is likely to be some time before many of your audience catch up with you, because they will spend at least some time pondering the item you have given them.

Advantages

- Models can show three-dimensional properties, and comparative sizes and shapes.

- Samples show actual properties; a sample is especially useful if you want to demonstrate the feel or the odour of something.

Disadvantages

- It is difficult to find and manoeuvre models that are big enough to show to large audiences.

- Models are distractions unless they are kept out of sight until they are needed, and are put away when they are finished with.

- The more intriguing the sample, the more distracting it is. Each member of the audience must have one to look at, and their examination of the sample must be carefully guided; but even careful guidance will not stop some of the audience ignoring what you are saying, while they study the sample, either on their own or in discussion with their neighbours.

Tips on planning

1. NEVER plan to hand round a single small model or sample. In addition to losing the attention of your audience, you are likely to have your model or sample returned to you in pieces. Engineers, in particular, like to take things apart to see how they work!

2. If you must hand out samples, be sure to have one for every member of your audience.

❑ Handouts: before, during or after a talk

It is possible to argue that a handout is the best visual aid. Each member of the audience can have a copy. He or she should have no difficulty in 'reading' it; he or she can write notes on it; he or she can take it away afterwards as a record of the information you presented in your talk.

However, the use of handouts raises three large questions:

- Is it best to distribute a full text of the talk, a synopsis or outline, a list of topics, or just individual pictures/diagrams/tables/charts?

- Is it best to distribute the handout(s) before, during, or after your talk?

- Is it desirable to use handouts *and* other types of visual aids during a talk?

My immediate answers to those questions are:

- rarely give out a full text: usually distribute an outline of your main points;
- distribute your handouts during your talk;
- use a combination of handouts and other visual aids.

Distribute a full text?

However, no over-all answers are possible. I think it is undesirable to give out a full text. If you give out a full text several days or weeks in advance of the meeting, you will find yourself in difficulty when you arrive to give your talk. You will find that your audience consists of:

- some who *have read* your text and *have brought it* with them;
- some who *have read* your text but *have not brought it* with them;
- some who *have not read* your text but *have brought it* with them;
- some who *have not read* your text and *have not brought it* with them.

How should you deal with such circumstances? If you give your talk as a development on the base material in your pre-distributed text, many of your audience are at a loss because they are not familiar with that base material. It is no good saying they have only themselves to blame for failing to read the text before they came to the meeting. The fact remains that they cannot understand some or all of your talk. However, if you present in your talk simply the same material as is in the pre-distributed paper, you insult and waste the time of those who have read your text in advance. You are in a dilemma that cannot be resolved in a way that is completely satisfactory for all your audience.

My advice would be that you *never* give out a complete text; but I am aware that there are circumstances in which that has to be done. For example, sometimes the organisers of an international symposium require you to send your text in advance, and it is included in a thick volume of 'proceedings' that is given out as delegates arrive; or your company sends a report or proposal to a client, and you then have to go to a follow-up meeting to 'speak to' the paper or proposal that has been distributed.

There are several possible ways of making the best of an unsatisfactory situation:

- you can plan a talk during which you take your audience into and out of the pre-distributed text when you need visual material or reference to calculations;

- you can plan a talk not using the pre-distributed text but issuing a further summary and/or set of key points on separate handouts — providing a 'working text' for the presentation;

- you can plan a talk not using the pre-distributed text but giving a summary and key points on slides, transparencies or other visual aids;

- you can plan a talk during which you use both the pre-distributed text and other visual aids.

In no circumstances should you *read* all or part of the pre-distributed text to your audience. That is especially offensive to those who have read it already. Your audience can read the text silently much faster than you can read it aloud; and reading aloud is an activity that requires special skill if it is to be done effectively.

Above all, make clear to your audience at the outset of the talk what you plan to do and how you want them to handle the pre-distributed text. For example:

> 'Ladies and gentlemen, you have been given a copy of my text, but as you have had little time to read it, I propose to begin by summarising my key findings, and then to highlight some of the implications for future work. I shall ask you from time to time to refer to my paper, to look at some of the illustrations there, but for the moment I should like to ask you to leave the text on one side while we review ...'

> 'Ladies and gentlemen, you have all received a copy of the proposal made by my company. In this follow-up talk, I should like to begin by highlighting our main proposals, and by emphasising the benefits that would stem from the choices we have offered you. To reduce the complexity of the material, I have prepared a handout/flip-chart/transparency outlining each choice. The material is the same as is in the proposal, but I thought it would be easier to use this/these 'working documents' during my presentation this morning.'

In other words, do everything possible to control the audience's handling of the pre-distributed text. Take them into and *out of* the text courteously. Ensure that there is no point at which they are uncertain where their focus of attention should be.

This last point is especially important if you produce additional handouts, transparencies, or other visual aids. When you use handouts of any sort, you automatically create a division of focus for the audience: should they look at you or at the handout? If they have a pre-distributed text, and then you present some slides or transparencies as well, they have three possible points of focus: you, the pre-distributed text, and the image on the screen. Wherever possible, avoid causing this three-way split; but if you do decide the three-way split is necessary, build into your talk plenty of guidance to the audience about where you want their attention concentrated. Give them plenty of guiding prompts such as:

> ...I should like you now to look at this OHP slide. It is the same diagram as in the pre-distributed text, so you need not turn to it there. On this slide, ...

> ...The five points I have just made were a quick summary of the problems we have to overcome. Would you now please turn to page 47 in the text you have received, and look at the two sets of figures presented there ...

> ...I'd like to leave those tables now, and I shall not refer to the text again for five minutes or so. I'd like you to join me in reflecting on the possible reaction from X if we were to ...

Prompts/instructions like these help the audience recognise what is expected of them, and give them time to assimilate and adjust to your material.

You must be careful to allow time: groups move slowly; you will probably need to repeat page numbers; you must always watch to see that they are all keeping up with you; and you must watch to see that you do not lose some of your audience in small, whispered discussions. The slight disturbances to concentration caused when you ask your audience to turn to a text are very likely to promote physical and intellectual 'bumping into' the person in the next seat. If discussion begins, you must decide quickly whether you want to harness it by asking the conversationalists to raise their point with the whole group, or whether you want to ask them to save the point for a later question-and-answer session by a comment such as:

> ...I know those figures provoke interesting discussion points I have not made so far, but I'd ask you to keep them for the question-and-answer session. In the meantime, ...

Previous distribution of a complete text before a talk creates so many difficulties that I recommend that you avoid doing so if at all possible. Are the difficulties reduced if you provide a complete text, but distribute it during or after the talk?

A complete text distributed after the talk is no longer an aid to the presentation of the talk. It may help the audience by providing easy retrieval of what you said, but it does not help them with the tasks of comprehending and assimilating what you say in your talk — which is the principal objective of introducing a visual aid.

I recognise that by telling your audience before the talk that a complete text will be handed out afterwards, you relieve them of the need to try to remember what you have said, and of the need to make notes. That advantage is probably outweighed by two disadvantages: one is that you discourage your audience from the activity of making notes, which is an activity that many people find a great help to getting items of information into focus and into their memories; the other is that a previously prepared text cannot take account of any impromptu variation in your presentation that you make in the light of the audience's response, nor can it record information that emerges in a question-and-answer session.

It is possible to distribute a complete text at some time during your talk, and to use it at that point, and subsequently, as an in-

104   Chapter 9

talk handout. At least in that way you can be sure that all the audience are in the same position — no-one has seen the text before your talk. Also, provided you plan carefully, you can be sure that everyone gets a copy (if you rely on using a pre-distributed text, *always* take some extra copies to give to members of the audience who have not brought their copies to the meeting).

The provision of the complete text gives the audience the best possible help with storage and retrieval of your information. Though the pre-printed text will not contain any of your impromptu remarks, or any information from the post-talk discussion, at least it gives a full and accurate record of most of what you said; and the audience can add some notes after you have given out the text.

These points seem to be advantages. The main weakness of all other forms of visual aids is that they give the audience at best limited help with the task of selecting and recording the main information in your presentation. Every experienced speaker knows that an audience's notes of what they *think* was said are frequently wildly different from what the speaker wished to convey!

There is no doubt that the provision of a full text to take away is a benefit to an audience (at least, they feel that it is, though my experience is that most of the paper handed out after talks is simply stored, unread, for a period, and then thrown away). But to give out a full text breaks one of the most important rules about the design of visual aids — that you should not distract your audience by providing information that you do not intend to mention (more detail in Chapter 11, page 140). If you give your audience a full text, and then ask them to refer just to parts of it, you will almost certainly find that some listeners cease to concentrate on what you are saying because they are browsing through the rest of the material in the text.

Alternatively, or additionally, you may be tempted to paraphrase or summarise parts of the text while the audience are looking at them. Never direct your audience's attention to a page, and then summarise what is on the page in different words, in a different order, or in different detail. By all means summarise one or more pages, but do so without suggesting that your audience should look at those pages. Do not confuse the listeners by saying:

> '... as you will see on pages 44 and 45, I have argued that ...'

and then summarising the argument in different words. That will leave them hurrying over the page, trying unsuccessfully to find the words you are using. The result will be confusion and exasperation. If you want the audience to read your argument, give them time to do so. Announce clearly what you want them to read, give time for reading, and then go on.

Distribute handout sheets during your talk?

In general, then, I am not in favour of using complete texts as handouts, either by pre-distribution or by distributing them during the talk. They have the virtue of being the most complete and accurate take-away material; but the operational problems of handling them successfully are so great that I prefer other forms of handouts — either outlines of the main points of a talk, or just individual items such as diagrams, charts or tables.

I make great use of handout sheets. I do so because I can have the greatest possible control over events if I have my support materials in handout form. During many years as an itinerant lecturer, I have suffered so often from poor equipment, and from the failure of lecture organisers to provide equipment, that I take handout material with me wherever possible. The lamp cannot fail in a pile of handouts! Handouts are not affected by the absence of a screen or plain wall on which to project slides. The use of handouts does not depend on the presence of a supply of chalk or of good black-out curtains. If I take a more-than-ample supply of handout sheets with me to a talk, I know that I have the provision of visual-aid material firmly under control, *and* I know that I am providing my audience with an accurate, take-away version of the most important material I want to present.

Of course, problems remain. To distribute an outline of the main points at the beginning of a talk is inevitably a distraction: it presents information that you will not discuss immediately, and it provides a piece of paper for people to fidget with. To overcome these problems as far as possible, it is desirable not to distribute a handout at the very beginning of a talk. First, establish rapport (with your introductory remarks), and then distribute your outline handout as part of your overview of what is to come. The outline handout then provides useful evidence of the pattern of information that the audience can expect, and you have a convenient moment at which to encourage them to add their own notes to the outline as the lecture progresses.

Another problem that you must consider is the size and arrangement of the audience. If you have 500 people arranged in long rows, 'theatre' style, the dissemination of your handouts will take time and cause disturbance. You will probably need assistants; and even with assistants, the time required for distribution will be substantial. You must not continue with the talk during the distribution.

The gap in your presentation caused by the distribution can be seen as a disadvantage; but it can also be seen as an advantage, because it gives the audience a chance to relax from careful listening for a moment or two — they have a chance physically and psychologically to make themselves comfortable before you start again.

Combine handouts and other visual aids?

To use handouts alone, though safe, is monotonous. There is no variation in mode of presentation throughout the talk. Also, it is difficult to guide your audience to specific items in your material. If you have a diagram, a calculation, or some text on a screen or board, you can focus or highlight by pointing at the item and using words such as:

This is the key number.

If you have to refer to a handout, you have to use words such as:

The fifth number on the third line, 453.7, is the key number.

For these reasons, it is usually wise to move away from handouts for some of the time during your presentation. You can do this by planning a short question-and-answer period, or by planning to use an OHP transparency or a flip-chart for a while. But if you do plan to introduce a transparency or a flip-chart, remember that you will divide focus (a problem discussed on page 102): you will have to guide your audience away from your handout to the other visual aid, and then guide them back to the handout when you want them to return to it.

Over-all possibilities for introducing handouts:

What?	*When?*
• A complete text	• In advance of your talk
• An outline of main topics/points	• Immediately before or at the start of your talk
• A text or illustration to support a single point	• During your talk
	• After your talk

Advantages

- If you give everyone a complete text, you can be sure they all have a record of exactly what you said.

- If you give everyone a copy of a handout, you can be sure that everyone can see the text or illustration clearly.

Disadvantages

- If you give everyone a complete text, you do not need to give a talk. The audience can read faster than you can speak.

- You cannot be sure that texts given out in advance will be read and/or brought to the meeting.

- A complete text given out immediately before or at the start of a talk cannot be absorbed immediately, and provides the audience with an alternative to listening to you.

- Handouts of any sort given *after* the talk are not visual aids to the presentation.

- Handouts given after the talk do not help the audience absorb and recall material from your impromptu answers to questions.

- Handouts of any sort are items for the audience to fidget with.

Handouts 109

Advantages (continued)

- Listeners do not have to make notes; they are free to concentrate on your argument.

- Listeners can make notes on their individual copies of the handouts.

- If you give out a handout during your talk, your listeners have a text to take away as an aid to recall, and you can be sure that the text represents accurately what you said.

- If you use handouts, you do not have to depend on the presence and reliability of electrical equipment.

- The gap in your presentation caused by the distribution of

Disadvantages (continued)

- Listeners are encouraged to listen passively; the activity of making notes helps to 'fix' points in the memory.

- Handouts, like all visual aids, give the audience an alternative point of focus (other than yourself). It is difficult to co-ordinate reading from a paper with watching and listening to a speaker (more difficult than looking at an on-screen image while watching and listening to a speaker who is standing close beside that image).

- Sets of handouts are bulky and heavy to carry; if you plan to give handouts to large groups, you need to recruit helpers.

- Distribution of handouts during a talk takes up

Advantages (continued)

handouts may be a useful interlude for the audience, giving a change of intensity and pace.

- An 'outline' handout, especially if it is laid out well, usefully emphasises the pattern of information you intend to go through (which is often particularly valuable during your opening overview of a presentation).

- Provision of a handout to illustrate or support a single point in your argument helps to emphasise that point.

Disadvantages (continued)

time, interrupts the audience's concentration on your argument, and may tempt people to begin conversations.

- A complete text or an 'outline' handout provides the audience with advance information, which may distract them from listening to your current point.

- Provision of 'single-point' handouts may over-emphasise the points supported or illustrated by those handouts; the rest of your talk, which is not supported by handouts, may — contrary to your intention — seem less significant.

- Use of handouts as the only form of aid is monotonous.

Especially good for:

- coping with circumstances in which you are unsure what equipment will be available at the venue for your talk;

- enabling the audience to take away accurate versions of complex information like calculations, architectural drawings, factory layouts;

- providing a convenient record not only of the key points of your presentation but also (occasionally and discreetly) correct details of your name, address, source materials, and other useful information.

Tips on planning

1. Ensure that you have a copy of every handout for every member of the audience, plus a few spares. Particularly, if you have to send your text in advance, have some spare copies available for the people who did not receive a copy or who have forgotten to bring it to the meeting.

2. If you plan to use handouts, ensure that you allow time for:
    - distribution;
    - reading and assimilation.

3. It is reasonably easy for the audience to change from distant focus on you, to distant focus on a screen or chart with you standing beside it. It requires more time and help from you for your audience to change from distant focus on you, to close focus on a sheet (and/or to find the place in a leaflet or complete text). You will probably need to hold up and point at the handout, to help people with orientation, and/or to give extra 'verbal pointers' — clear instructions about where to look.

4. Do not read aloud the text that your audience are reading on your handout *unless* you want to give special stress to certain words or points by intonation, and/or you want to stop and make a point about the way in which the text is worded.

5. If you introduce OHP transparencies as well as handouts, to relieve the monotony of using handouts as the only form of visual aid, be careful not to ask your audience to cope simultaneously with three (or more) points of focus (you, the handout, and the transparency). Guide them carefully from focus to focus by words and gestures, and allow time for switching.

6. Use coloured paper as colour-coding if you have many handouts. Help by numbering the handouts, either in advance or as you distribute them.

7. Sometimes, deliberately leave gaps on your handout, and then encourage the audience to write down specific points as you make them; even dictate specific words or numbers.

8. If you (have to) give out a complete text, and then talk about more information than is on the text, you must tell the audience that you are doing so, and:

- give them a chance to record the new information;
- or • give them additional handouts;
- and/or • give them reference sources for the new information.

Do not leave them feeling angry or cheated that the new information is not in your text.

❑ 35mm-slide projectors

Since most 35mm slides are made professionally, they usually look good — their lettering is sharp, the colour is clear, they have a professional appearance. They can therefore be valuable complements to a talk. But the introduction of a 35mm projector causes even more problems than the introduction of an overhead projector, so at least until some of the operating problems are

35mm-slide projectors 113

overcome, I recommend that you are wary of choosing to use 35mm slides.

Let me emphasise that in a large auditorium they are often essential, because you cannot obtain a large enough image with any other equipment. At the other end of the audience-size scale, for a group up to about 10, use of slides in a modern projector-monitor unit (like a small television set, with a carousel on top) can be very effective, especially since the unit can be used in full room-lighting. But the size of projector-monitor screens is not adequate to permit use of those units for larger groups. Also, the cost of making slides is still higher than most organisations are willing to contemplate for 'run-of-the-mill' presentations. We are still waiting for equipment that will make the production and use of 35mm slides a more competitive option for most presentation-makers.

Advantages

- Slides made professionally usually have high qualities of lettering, drawing and colour.

- Given a sufficiently powerful projector, you can fill a large screen with your images, and have the projector outside the lecture-room (in a 'projection box') or at the back of the room, thereby

Disadvantages

- The use of a slide projector still usually requires the darkening of the room, often complete darkness, before the images are really clear. The changeover is itself a disturbance to the audience's concentration on the message.

- Breakdown of the machinery brings the presentation to a complete halt.

Advantages (continued)

reducing the disturbance created by the machinery itself.

Disadvantages (continued)

- It is difficult to plan any change of mode in the presentation, because moving from darkness to light and then back again is undesirably disruptive.

- Once you have your slides in a tray or carousel, and you have begun your presentation, it is difficult to change your scheme if feedback from the audience suggests you should do so.

- In the gloom or darkness, it is difficult to get any feedback from your audience, or to create any sense of contact at all.

- In gloom or darkness, it is difficult or impossible for the audience to make notes.

- The slides become the principal visual focus. You are relegated to an accompanying (often disembodied) voice. It

Disadvantages (continued)

is usually impossible to arrange any variation in visual focus.

❑ A slide-based presentation in the dark *is* soporific.

Once again, most of these disadvantages are operational; but they are much more difficult to overcome than the disadvantages of using an overhead projector. Given good equipment that requires the lighting only to be reduced, not extinguished, and given careful preparation and rehearsal, a slide-based presentation can be very effective. I have to say, though, that I have suffered through so many droning, relentless catalogues of 'This slide shows .....' that I urge beginners to think very hard before choosing to introduce slides as their visual aids.

Tips on planning

1. If you plan to use slides, try to plan a reasonably substantial opening section *without slides* in which you establish rapport with your audience. Try not to put the lights out too soon.

2. If you need to compare and contrast material frequently, and the material will not fit comfortably on one slide, consider using two projectors (if the equipment is available).

3. If you have two projectors available, you can also consider (*very carefully*!) superimposing one image on another, to help with discussion of changes or of comparisons and contrasts.

4. If you want to repeat a slide, do NOT run back through the carousel: have a repeat slide.

5. If you want to have a period in which you simply talk to the audience without a slide on the screen, do not simply leave an empty space in the carousel, which produces an empty, glaring screen: include a blank slide made to produce a restful pastel colour on the screen. But beware of leaving your audience looking at nothing for long: either move into view yourself somehow, or provide a slide for them to look at.

6. Plan your presentation so that your words and slides are synchronised. Do not begin talking about a new point while a slide relevant to the previous point remains on the screen; and do not put up a slide relating to a new point but continue talking about points illustrated by the previous slide.

7. Wherever possible, design a focusing technique into the slides themselves; do not rely on using a pointer, or a torch that projects an arrow on to the screen. If you use a pointer, you will often find yourself walking about in the beam of light from the projector, with the image projected distractingly on your body. If you use an arrow-torch, you will find it almost impossible to point steadily at a chosen item on the screen (see the warning on page 130). A well-designed slide should have only one point of focus anyway. Bolding and colour can help to draw the readers' attention to the desired principal focus. If necessary, you can have an arrow printed on the slide to show the item on which you wish to concentrate attention. Perhaps best of all, use a sequence of slides to emphasise different elements in a single picture during your discussion.

❑ Filmstrips, film loops and films

Filmstrips are effectively sets of slides in fixed strips. All the discussion of the use of slides applies equally to the use of filmstrips.

Film loops and films take over completely from the presenter for a period. They remain aids to the total presentation, but while they are in progress, the speaker might as well not be there.

That is not to say that you should never consider including a film in your presentation. It does mean that you have to think carefully whether you are going to construct an argument into which you can fit a short film as an element, or whether the film will itself seem of such substance that you should plan simply an introduction and conclusion to it.

It may be effective to plan an introduction of some length, in which you establish your objective, and perhaps alert the audience to what is coming and what you want them to look for. However, recognise that well-made films usually come to a firm end, often literally with words and music designed for effect. If you try to go on at length after the film, it is likely that your efforts will seem anticlimactic. Usually, the best you can hope to arrange after a film is a question-and-answer session or a discussion.

Much depends on the length and type of film, and on your intentions. If you face a teaching task, and if the film is short enough, you can plan to show the film twice: you can prepare the ground briefly; show the film; highlight and discuss points; then show the film again.

You can also use a silent film, and present a commentary yourself; but the art of providing a 'voice over' takes considerable learning: scripting and timing need great care. If you are going to consider going to such lengths, you would possibly do better to consider using a videotape.

❑ Videotapes

Videotapes share most of the qualities of films, but have one great difference: they can be stopped, enabling you to talk about a still, though often flickering, image; they can also be re-wound and re-run for emphasis and review.

Advantages

- You can capture on videotapes the movement and flow of activities and processes, which you cannot re-create in still images on slides or transparencies.

- You can make videotapes yourself (though for important presentations, it is desirable to use a professional production team, familiar with story-boards, camera angles, cutting, splicing and dubbing).

- Videotapes can have all the aesthetic qualities of professionally made slides, transparencies or films.

Disadvantages

- To get an image large enough for a large group, you must use elaborate projection equipment that is costly and not often available.

- If you use multiple small monitors, your audience may lose some of their sense of unity as they gather into small groups; and you may have difficulty physically and psychologically reconstituting the over-all group (if you want to) after you have shown the tape.

- Production of a good videotape calls for considerable planning and resources.

Videotapes 119

Advantages (continued)

- You can stop a videotape, and talk about a still, though sometimes flickering image; you can re-wind the tape, and re-run sections for emphasis and review.

Disadvantages (continued)

- If you use multiple monitors, it is not easy to point to items on the screen.

- For large-screen presentations, it is usually necessary to darken the room, with all the attendant disadvantages of doing so.

Especially useful for:

- illustrating activities and processes;

- introducing people into your visual material (to introduce people into still photographs on slides or transparencies often seems forced; there is still a possibility of creating an artificial atmosphere if you put people into your video-recording, but there is a much greater chance of bringing your visual material alive by showing people working and talking naturally).

Tips on planning

1. As in the use of slides, plan to make yourself the central focus of the audience's attention for at least a reasonable time at the start, to establish rapport, and to set the objectives and tone of the event.

2. Plan carefully the location you and your recorder will

120   Chapter 9

occupy in relation to the screen, so that you can control comfortably any stopping and re-running you wish to do, *and* can comfortably point out on the screen anything you wish to highlight.

3. Plan what you will say about the video with as much selectivity and attention to time as you would if you were planning to talk about 'still' visual aids. Beware of being tempted to extemporise.

❑ Closed-circuit television

When you use closed-circuit television, a camera focuses on you and the material you wish to display, and transmits 'live' pictures to your audience through monitors. From the speaker's point of view, preparation of the talk goes on mainly as if the presentation were to be made directly to the audience. A choice of which aids to use — charts, slides or transparencies — still has to be made. The main difference is that it becomes possible to contemplate showing your audience very small objects and small-scale activities: you can consider demonstrating a small experiment on a bench before a large audience, and the charts and drawings you plan to use can be relatively small. The critical factors affecting your decisions about legibility become the power of the camera and the size of the monitors.

Presentations using closed-circuit television have to be seen as substantial 'productions', with detailed planning not only of your talk but also of camera angles, lighting, and the placing of microphones. You need people to operate the camera(s), and you need time to rehearse if the presentation is to run smoothly. These are substantial extra requirements, but essentially the business of planning your talk remains as we have discussed previously.

There is inevitably distraction created by the paraphernalia you must use. There is inevitably loss of contact between yourself and the audience, who must focus on the monitors. There are, however, undoubted gains in some circumstances — for instance, in ability to show surgery in progress, or ability to show immediate effects of adding one chemical to another in a small test-tube.

For most of us, though, the opportunity to use closed-circuit television does not exist. We must plan to use commonly available equipment.

❏ Audio Aids

The main audio aids we can consider using are record-players, compact-disc players, and tape-recorders.

It should go without saying that audibility for *all* the audience is vital; but I have suffered many times from infuriating speakers who have said: 'I doubt if you'll be able to hear this clearly, but this is a recording of ...'!

A clear, audible recording can bring considerable benefits to a talk. Consider the possibility of giving a talk about birdsong or about local dialects *without* a recording. But it is wise to keep extracts from recordings reasonably short. Audiences sometimes have difficulty in keeping their attention on a disembodied voice or other sound. They feel the lack of a point of visual focus. They are tempted to focus on you, the presenter of the over-all 'show', and are distracted by observing how *you* are reacting to the recording, when they should be formulating their own response without influence from you. Music, somehow, is easier to attend to without a visual focus; but recorded extracts included in a talk should normally be kept brief, especially if they are included to illustrate an argument. If the extract goes on too long, your audience may find they cannot remember the threads of the argument prior to your introduction of the recording.

It is possible to synchronise a tape-recording with 35mm slides, creating a 'tape-slide' presentation. Such presentations can be professionally prepared, and can have considerable impact on an audience. But to use a tape-slide show is to abandon all pretence that *you* are giving a talk. As with a film, while the tape-slide show is in progress, the speaker might just as well not be there. A tape-slide presentation *replaces* rather than *aids* a speaker. Also, videotapes, film loops and short films can now be made almost as cheaply as a tape-slide presentation, and are free from the possibilities of technical hitches that accompany tape-slide presentations.

❑ Multi-media

In a multi-media presentation, elements from a variety of electronic media are combined into a computer-controlled production. Text, graphics, video material, sound recordings — any material that can be stored electronically in digital form in a database — can be included. The visual material can be projected on to large screens, not just on to television monitors.

At present, however, multi-media presentations are complicated and expensive to produce. Substantial professional knowledge and equipment are needed. Professional skills are needed for compiling databases, accessing and co-ordinating the chosen mixed materials, and producing the finished presentation. Also, like films and tape-slide presentations, multi-media productions usually replace rather than aid a speaker. For the moment, therefore, if you are an 'occasional' presenter, consider using multi-media only if you have a very special 'show' to produce, and if you have experts available to help with both production and presentation of that show.

CHAPTER 10

Handling visual-aid equipment

The need for foresight

Like everything else connected with effective speaking, the handling of visual aids needs to be thought through carefully. Be methodical. Think out in advance:

- Which visual aid(s) shall I use?
- When?
- What will that involve?

Try to foresee every movement you will have to make as you present your talk. One of the chief sources of speakers' anxiety is fear of the unexpected. Think through the whole 'event' *in detail*. By doing so, you will minimise the likelihood of something unexpected happening.

In the first half of this chapter, my principal advice will be on positioning and movement — on tactics for making yourself and your audience as comfortable as possible during your presentation, especially while you use visual-aid equipment. In the second half, I shall discuss tactics for planning the words you will use as you manipulate the equipment. Then, in the following chapter, I shall discuss tactics of design — tactics for creating visual materials for display on your chosen equipment.

Viewing and arranging the room

Find out in advance as much as possible about the venue for your presentation. I recognise that, if you are going to address a

124 Chapter 10

potential customer overseas, learning about the venue may not be easy; but even when you have to plan for a new and distant context, it is usually possible to have at least a brief telephone conversation about the probable size and composition of the audience, the layout of the conference room, and the equipment available. Do everything possible to reduce the possibility of being surprised and worried when you eventually walk into the venue for your presentation.

Ideally, organise the layout of the room yourself, especially the arrangement of *your* space — the area around the table or lectern, with its blackboard/whiteboard, projector, flip-chart, or other equipment.

Do you plan to use a blackboard or whiteboard? If so, will it be movable or fixed? Will it be large enough for you to plan to use separate areas — an area for a cumulative summary, an area for putting up key words or figures, and a 'working surface' for on-the-spot calculations? If not, will there be a flip-chart that you can use for your cumulative summary or your key words?

Will there be a supply of chalk and/or flip-chart pens (pens that are not dried up!)? Be prepared: take some with you, in case there is no supply!

If you plan to use a blackboard/whiteboard *and* a projector (for 35mm slides or for overhead-projector transparencies) will the board be accessible at the same time as the screen? An astonishing number of conference rooms have screens that drop down in front of the board, making it impossible to use both at the same time.

Is the flip-chart flat against a wall, making the 'flipping over' of charts impossible, or at least awkward? If the flip-chart is on a movable stand, is it placed where you want it (depending on whether you are right-handed or left-handed)? If you plan to use

Viewing and arranging the room 125

a flip-chart and a projector, are the chart-stand and the screen conveniently placed for you to move between them, and for your audience to see both clearly? If not, and if you can get into the room well before the presentation, move the equipment and/or the audience's seats into the best possible configuration.

If you are to speak at a venue away from your home base, always ask if you can look at the venue well before the presentation is scheduled to begin, so that, if necessary, you can move things into more convenient positions, or at least think of changes to your plans in the light of what you have seen.

Make a calm and methodical appraisal of the room *before* you start. If you plan to use an overhead projector, will you be more comfortable with it on the left or on the right of your lectern or table? If necessary (and, of course, if possible without inconveniencing others), move the table and/or the projector before you start.

Be methodical. Minimise the likelihood that, when the time comes for your presentation, you will be confronted by a feature of the physical arrangements that will cause you to be surprised and flustered. Think about the lectern or table. Plan how you will arrange your notes and materials on it. Plan to have a space for notes, a space for overhead transparencies that are waiting to be shown (face upwards), and a space for transparencies you have used and will not want again (face down):

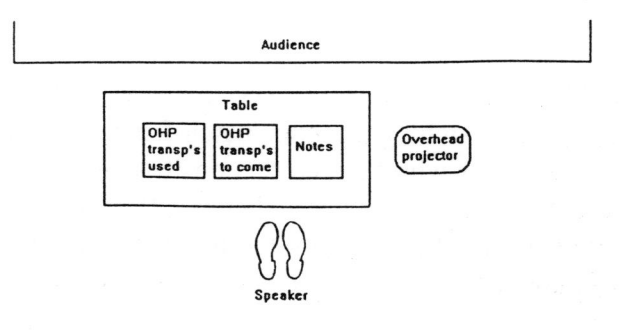

Write notes on one side of your paper only, and number the pages. If you want to use the same drawing or photograph at different points in your talk, have a repeat slide or chart: never put yourself at the disadvantage of having to rummage in your pile of used transparencies or papers for material you used earlier.

Choosing where to stand

If you plan to show material on a board, flip-chart, or screen, think about where you will stand while you talk about the material on the display surface. Too many speakers take up a position that I call the 'Wimbledon spectator' position — midway between the table and the display surface, sideways on to the audience:

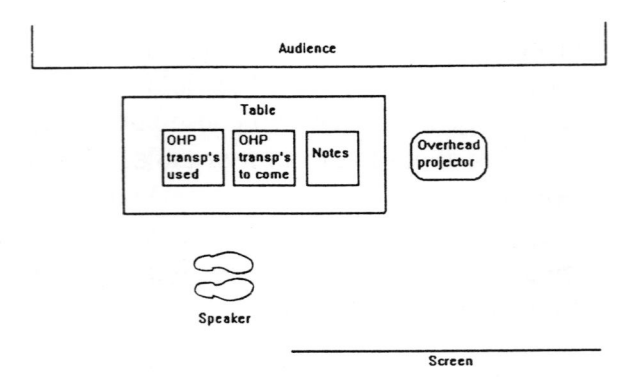

In this position, the speaker is obliged to swing his/her head from side to side, as if watching a tennis match from a central position. In practice, speakers who take up this position spend more time looking at the screen than at the audience. If you do that, you lose eye-contact, and thereby lose the feedback that is essential if you are to judge how well your talk is being understood.

Choosing where to stand   127

Preferably, when you wish to talk about material on a screen or board, take up a position beside the display surface (to the left or to the right, depending on whether you are right- or left-handed):

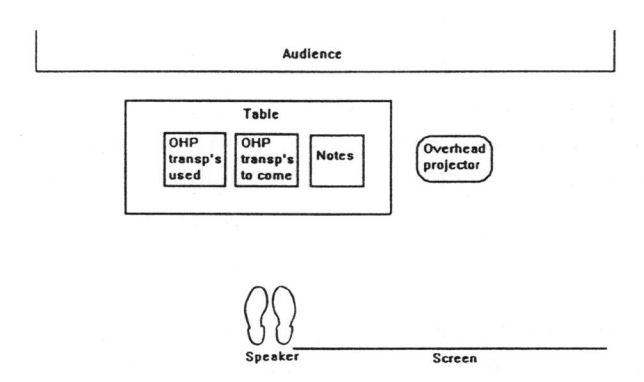

```
┌─────────────────────────────────────────┐
│              Audience                    │
└─────────────────────────────────────────┘
              ┌─────────────────────┐
              │       Table         │
              │ ┌────┐┌────┐        │
              │ │OHP ││OHP │ Notes  │ ┌─────────┐
              │ │tran││tran│        │ │Overhead │
              │ │sp's││sp's│        │ │projector│
              │ │used││to  │        │ └─────────┘
              │ │    ││come│        │
              │ └────┘└────┘        │
              └─────────────────────┘

               ◯◯
             ─────────────────────────────
              Speaker        Screen
```

From this position, you can point at the display surface easily, and yet remain facing your audience most of the time, maintaining good eye-contact.

If you are uneasy about moving back beside the display surface without your notes, take the notes with you. Alternatively, if you are using a flip-chart, you can write your notes lightly in pencil on the top corner of your flip-chart pad, where *you* can see them but your audience cannot.

A position beside the display surface has another major advantage: you and the display surface constitute a single area of focus; if you take up a Wimbledon-spectator position, your audience has two areas of focus competing for attention — you and the display:

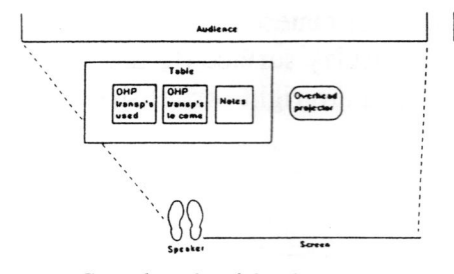

128 Chapter 10

Speaker beside the screen: audience have a single area to focus on.

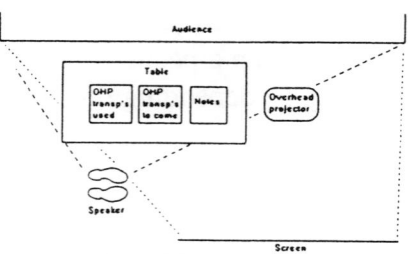

Speaker in the 'Wimbledon' position: audience have two separate points of focus

A position beside the display surface is usually essential if you are using an overhead projector. In theory, when you use an overhead projector, you should be able to remain at your lectern or table, facing your audience, with your visual material projected *overhead*. Also in theory, you should be able to write on a transparency during your talk, and you should be able to point easily at parts of the image on the transparency, without getting yourself silhouetted on the screen. In practice, however, most conference rooms do not allow for *overhead* projection. The screen is free-standing on a tripod, or is fixed to a wall, in a position that ensures that you or the projector obstruct the view of some or all of your audience some or all of the time. In particular, when you write on a transparency during the lecture, or if you stand beside the projector to point at parts of the image on the transparency, you block the view for some of the audience:

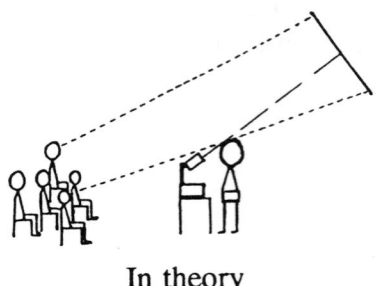

In theory 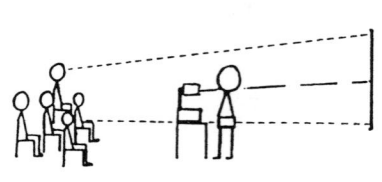   In practice

Regrettably, therefore, the overhead projector cannot conveniently be used as it is designed to be used. You must plan to keep out of the audience's sight-lines as much as possible. This means you must do your pointing on the surface of the screen itself, being careful to keep out of the light from the projector as much as possible.

Pointing

Pointing is valuable to help your audience focus quickly on the area of your visual that you wish to discuss. Do not rely only on vague expressions such as 'As you can see ...' or 'Note that ...'. Show your audience *where* they can see what you want them to see. Point slowly and deliberately, remembering that your audience will need a little longer than you do to arrive at the spot you are indicating. Preferably, use a pointer, BUT:

- don't fidget with the pointer, especially if it is one of the retracting type, while you are not pointing with it;
- don't brandish the pointer at the audience, or emulate an orchestral conductor;
- don't stand in the Wimbledon-spectator position, flapping the pointer vaguely in the direction of the screen.

When you are not actually using the pointer, put it down.

Remember to remain facing the audience while you are pointing at any display surface, and point with the arm nearest the surface:

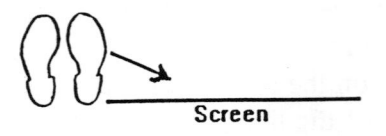

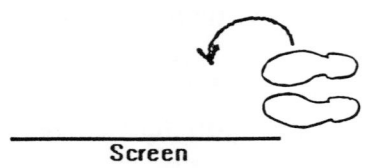

Point with your
'inside' arm

Don't point with your
'outside' arm

If you turn sideways to the display surface and the audience, and point with your outside arm, you will find yourself either talking to the display surface, or talking over your shoulder to an audience that is gazing at your back and ear.

Guiding your audience around a screen is especially difficult if you are addressing a very large group, or if you are seated at a computer keyboard, projecting images on to a large screen through an overhead projector. In a large hall, you will need a large screen, and probably you will need an especially powerful overhead projector or a 35mm-slide projector. When your screen is 10 feet x 10 feet (approximately 3 metres x 3 metres) or more, it is difficult to reach all areas of the display from one position, even with a long pointer. There is no easy way to overcome this difficulty.

If you have to work in a darkened room, using a 35mm-slide projector, you may be offered a hand-held 'torch' which projects an arrow on to the screen. I would warn you to experiment thoroughly with it before you use it in your presentation. I have never seen an 'arrow torch' used successfully: that is, I have never seen a speaker with a hand steady enough to move and hold the arrow without distracting wobbles.

A long pointer may be available. Long pointers, too, are difficult to handle steadily. Also, as the screen becomes larger and the pointer longer, the speaker begins to seem incongruously diminutive beside the large image on the screen.

Perhaps the best way to cope with large-screen images is to build cues, indicators, and highlights into the design of your transparencies and slides wherever possible. In Chapter 11, I shall suggest that arrows, numbers, boxes, colour, and other highlighting devices may be useful means of helping your audience focus on and move around your visual material. If you have to work with a large screen, consider preparing sequences of slides in circumstances where you might otherwise prepare just one. Instead of struggling to guide your audience to half-a-dozen significant areas of a single slide, consider preparing half-a-dozen slides showing the same outline material, but with a different area highlighted on each slide in the sequence.

If you are seated at a computer keyboard, controlling a sequence of computer 'screens' that is being projected on to another display surface, it will be distracting for the audience, and probably unsettling for you as a keyboard operator, if you have to keep standing up to point at the larger display. To avoid this distraction, you can perhaps use the same highlighting tactics as I have just suggested for use with large-hall audiences. Alternatively, consider asking a colleague to operate the keyboard or to handle the pointer while you give the address.

Consider asking a colleague to help with *any* type of presentation. A joint presentation, well rehearsed, can often run with a variety and smoothness that is hard to achieve in a one-person presentation.

Leading with words

When the moment comes at which you want to put material on a board, or show a chart, transparency, or slide, always 'lead' with words. That is, before you show your visual material, tell the audience what to expect.

As you reveal your flip-chart, or as you switch on the projector, *you* know what is coming; *you* know how you are expected to 'read' the visual material that is about to appear. Put your audience as nearly as possible in the same position, by making an introductory, 'orientation' statement. Without such a statement, no matter how well designed your visual material may be, there will be a momentary uncertainty in your audience as they see the image on the screen, and try to discern what it signifies. Their eyes will rapidly 'search' the visual material for meaning. They will do this much faster than you can produce your first few words. Accordingly, it helps them focus, and it helps you guide their comprehension, if you tell them what you want them to see when the image appears.

Of course, once the image is revealed, your control over what the audience looks at is reduced. Of course, too, there may be occasions when you plan deliberately to surprise. Usually, however, you will want to keep your audience's concentration on the flow of ideas you have established previously. You will want them to interpret your visual material in a certain way, and to connect the new visual information with the words and images they have received so far. So, in your orientation remarks, connect what is coming with what has gone before, and direct attention to the point or feature you want the audience to focus on in the visual. For example:

> ... To illustrate that layout, here's an example from our factory at X. When you see the transparency, note how the main entrance, marked in green, is placed near ...

> ... I'm going to make four points about the engine: the first about the design of the turbine; the second about its fuel-consumption; the third about noise levels; and the fourth

about maintainability. First, the design of the turbine. On this slide, you will see at the front of ...

Leading with words is important to establish coherence in your talk. It also has a practical value in that your words fill the awkward silences that frequently occur when speakers use an overhead projector.

Probably, you have seen poorly prepared presentations that are embarrassing stop-go sequences. The speaker finishes what he/she has to say about one transparency. There is then a silence as he/she takes that transparency off the projector, finds the next one, places it on the projector, turns and looks at the image on the screen with an expression that seems to say: 'What on earth was I going to say about that?', and then resumes talking. During that period, the audience have nothing to do except watch the speaker manipulating the transparencies. Connecting comments, leading into the next visual, remove awkward silences, and create an atmosphere of confidence and control.

Handling the overhead projector

Handle the overhead projector calmly and skilfully. Always find the on/off switch before you start. (You may think that is an unnecessary piece of advice: but I have seen so many speakers thrown out of their stride for a few moments by their embarrassing inability to switch on the projector, that I include it here as something you should check.) Also before you start, ensure that the projector is correctly focused (use a spare transparency or put a coin on the glass plate, and ensure that its image on the screen is sharply focused). When you come to use your first transparency, put the transparency on the projector plate, and begin your orientation statement *before* you switch on the machine, thus avoiding even momentary glare from an unfilled screen.

In handling subsequent transparencies, you will be faced with a dilemma over whether or not to switch the projector off each time you have finished discussing a transparency. If you have a sequence of transparencies to show, constant switching on and off will be irritating to your audience and to you; but if you talk for long without a transparency on the projector, your audience will be dazzled by the bright, blank screen. How long is 'for long'? I can offer only a rough guide: probably, about 30 seconds.

Word:image mismatching

However, here is an important warning: don't be tempted to avoid the on-off problem by leaving a transparency on the screen after you have finished talking about it, and don't be tempted to put up the next transparency before you are ready to begin talking about it. For maximum effect, your words and your on-screen images must complement one another. Word:image mismatching distracts and confuses. An 'old' visual will be an unnecessary distraction from the new topic your words are introducing; a 'new' visual that appears before you begin to talk about it will distract your audience from your current words as they wonder: 'What does this new visual signify?', and 'Why has it appeared now?'

Word:image mismatching is a common fault in presentations based entirely on 35mm slides. A major disadvantage of 35mm-slide presentations is that room lights have to be dimmed or switched off. It is then impractical to have a pause between slides that is filled only by words from the speaker. Something has to be on the screen, or the screen remains a bright blank, or the room lights have to be switched back on. Many speakers overcome (or rather, ignore) this difficulty by leaving an 'old' slide on the screen while they move to another point in their discourse, or they put up a 'new' slide before they are ready to discuss it. Both steps are distracting for the audience. If you have to make a presentation based on 35mm slides, plan to co-ordinate your words and your slides exactly.

Plan *exactly* when you will reveal visual material, and when you will remove it. Keep covered, and/or out of sight, charts, models, or other visual material until the moment at which you wish to use it. When you have finished with it, remove it from view to minimise the possibility of word:image mismatch. The only exception to this rule is a cumulative summary that you build alongside the material you show on your main display surface.

By now, you will have recognised the objectives and the value of thinking through your talk *in detail* in advance. At the beginning of this chapter, I urged you to try to foresee every move you will have to make in your presentation. In Chapter 7, I urged you to include in your notes not only reminders of the subject-matter you want to cover but also reminders of when and how to handle your visual-aid equipment. The aim of all this is to reduce your chances of becoming flustered because something has happened that you did not expect. Certainly, detailed forward thinking takes time; and certainly, there will be occasions on which things happen that you did not foresee; but in my experience, time spent in thinking through the event that is to take place brings dividends in increased confidence and more competent presentation.

CHAPTER 11

General advice on designing 'visual' material for use in presentations

Helping your audience SEE what you mean

General advice

This chapter gives *general* advice on the design of 'visual' material — images, plans, diagrams, charts — that are to be displayed on flipcharts, overhead projectors, or other visual-aid equipment. To give *detailed* advice on the design of all types of tables, charts, or illustrations would occupy more pages than I have filled so far. For example, the detailed advice that I usually recommend fills **two** books. Both are by Edward Tufte: *Envisioning Information* and *The Visual Display of Quantitative Information* (both published by Graphics Press UK, PO Box 8, Godalming, Surrey, GU7 3HB). So, since my purpose is to produce a book on presentations that includes advice on the design of visuals, not a book on the design of visuals that includes advice on presentations, this chapter offers just general guidelines to have in mind when you sit down to manipulate your on-line graphics package or your hand-held coloured pens.

Good visual material helps your audience do two things: it helps them *focus* on what you are saying and *remember* what you have said. The primary objective of a visual is to help your audience with immediate *focusing* and *comprehending* during your talk. A secondary, though scarcely less important, objective is to help them with *remembering*, both while the talk is in progress, and after the presentation is finished. Design your visuals with both objectives in mind.

Statement visuals and illustration visuals

As you design your visuals, you will recognise that there are two broad types:

- **statement visuals** — visuals that *make a point*, that positively *show* relationships, contrasts, or features;

- **illustration visuals** — visuals that *make available an image* of something like an object, a circuit, an apparatus, or a plant layout, and *serve as a basis for detailed commentary* by the speaker.

In general, your audience should be able to *see* immediately the point you are making with a statement visual. Nevertheless, it is good tactics to reinforce your point with a clear caption, such as is provided in Figure 1, and by 'leading into' your visual with carefully planned orientation remarks (as discussed in Chapter 10, pages 131–133).

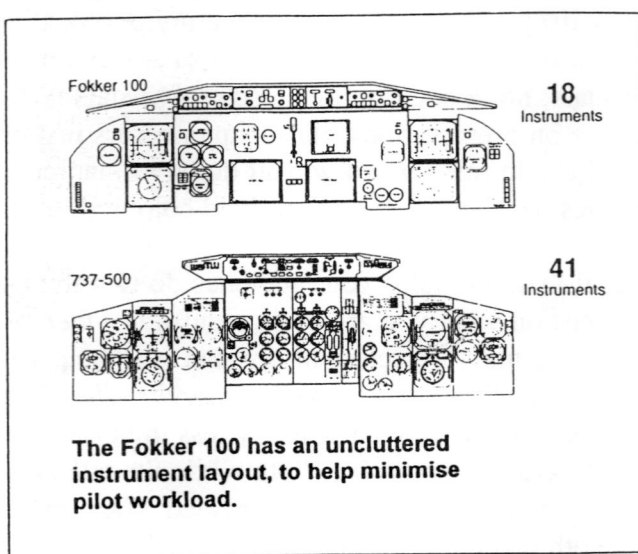

Figure 1. A 'statement visual', making a point: two instrument layouts are shown, to contrast the 'uncluttered' layout of the Fokker 100's instrument panel with that of its rival, the Boeing 737-500. The contrast is highlighted by the caption.

Statement visuals and illustration visuals 139

In an illustration visual, your aim may be simply to show what something looks like. In a presentation aimed at introducing a new control panel, the photograph of the panel in Figure 2a would show its appearance very satisfactorily; but it would be valuable to ask yourself: '*Why* am I showing what it looks like? Could I also make a point about it?'. As a broad generalisation, each visual should contribute something to the audience's greater understanding of your theme or argument: illustration visuals should not be introduced just for decorative effect. The illustration in Figure 2b also shows what the panel looks like, but the addition of the hand adds points about the instrument's size and portability.

Figure 2a.
An 'illustration visual', simply showing what an instrument looks like.

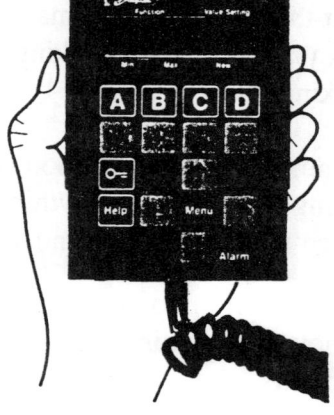

Figure 2b.
An 'illustration visual' that does more than show what the instrument looks like: it also makes points about size and portability.

An illustration visual may also make available an image (for example, a circuit diagram, an architect's drawing, or an aerial photograph of a plant layout) which the speaker can use to support explanation of the design, construction, or use of the item illustrated. The design and use of this type of visual needs care: exclude from your design any details you do not want or need to discuss; and try to ensure that your audience's attention to the visual stays related to the words they hear from you while your visual is displayed.

Controlling your audience's reading of your visual

As you design your visual, do not include any details that you do not want to discuss and/or that your audience do not need to see. If you plan to use an existing photograph or drawing, blank out unwanted or unnecessary elements. Unexplained details distract the audience, and may cause their attention to wander, so that they are no longer looking at the area of the visual that you are talking about.

To minimise the likelihood of such a word:image mismatch occurring, plan to do everything possible to control your audience's movement around your visual:

- Consider announcing (briefly) in your orientation 'lead-in' how many points you intend to make, the essence of those points, and which will be the first point/feature you want the audience to attend to.

- Consider the possibility of putting numbers on the visual to stress the sequence in which you want to focus on particular areas.

- Consider using several copies of the same visual, with different captions, and/or with boxes, arrows, or other highlighting devices drawing attention to different areas of the visual. (This tactic is probably the most useful aid to recall: otherwise, your audience have only a single visual image, with a single caption, to help with recall of the several points you made while that image was on the screen.)

- At least, plan to point firmly and deliberately to the area you are discussing.

No doubt, once you reveal the visual, some members of the audience will 'escape' from your control, and begin to look at areas of the visual you are not discussing at the moment; but if they become lost or confused after all your efforts to help them, they will have only themselves to blame.

The visual impact of words and numbers

To help with focusing and remembering, each visual should have an immediate and memorable visual quality— a distinctive shape, pattern, colour, or prominent feature. I am well aware that this requirement condemns the use of the 'word visuals' and 'number visuals' so often used by presenters of technical information. We must recognise, however, that words and numbers have little visual impact by themselves. To help with focusing and remembering, they need to be arranged in distinctive patterns, not in standard paragraphs or tables, which all look unmemorably alike.

Words by themselves have distinctive shapes; but when they are strung out in lines, they lose much of their visual distinctiveness and immediacy of impact; and when several lines are combined into a rectangular paragraph, there is little shape or pattern to help with focusing or recalling. From a distance — that is, from where your audience are sitting — one paragraph has much the same outline as another. If words are to be immediately effective, they need to be presented in varying patterns, with careful use of indentation, variation of fonts, variation of size, bolding, italics, and other visual cues for your audience. Consider the relative effectiveness of the rectangular, eight-line paragraph and the six-line 'bulleted' notes in Figures 3 and 4.

> **NEWDRUG**
>
> **ONE-TABLET-A-DAY DOSAGE**
>
> A single daily dose of NEWDRUG provides 24-hour blood pressure control. The recommended initial dose is a single 50 mg tablet. If optimal response is not achieved, the dosage should be increased to NEWDRUG 100 mg given as one-tablet-a-day. Full response is obtained within two weeks. Development of therapeutic tolerance has not been reported after long-term use.

Figure 3. An unhelpful 'word visual': a rectangular block that gives the audience no help with focusing or remembering by its layout or wording.

> **NEWDRUG**
>
> Dosage: one tablet a day
>
> - Single dose controls blood pressure for 24 hours
>   - Initial dose: 1 x 50 mg tablet daily
>   - If response is poor: increase dose to 1 x 100 mg tablet daily
> - Full response within two weeks
> - No reports of build-up of tolerance

Figure 4. A helpful 'word visual': both its layout and its wording help the audience with focusing and remembering.

Numbers similarly lack immediate visual effect. Numbers are all the same height and much the same shape. If I write that the number of units produced by a factory in four consecutive years was 48, 543, 299, and 338, you will have to go through two mental operations — first perceiving and then interpreting — to recognise which was the best year's output. If I give you the following bar chart, you get an immediate visual impression of the best year:

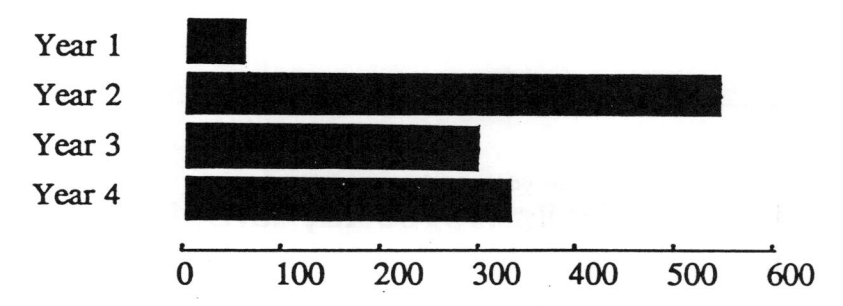

Year 1	▮
Year 2	▮▮▮▮▮▮▮▮▮▮
Year 3	▮▮▮▮▮
Year 4	▮▮▮▮▮▮

0   100   200   300   400   500   600

Of course, there will be occasions when there is no picture, diagram, or chart that you can use to help your audience focus on and remember an abstract concept you wish to discuss or a theoretical point you wish to make. There will also be occasions when you wish to discuss precise numbers, or present tabulations, or show exact formulae or equations. On those occasions, you will be obliged to use words, numbers, or tables in your visuals; but try always to use devices of layout to help your audience distinguish and recall the content of each visual.

Avoiding overload

Make maximum use of shape and pattern in your visuals; but keep them clear and uncomplicated: avoid the visual equivalent of verbosity. If you do want to make several related points, don't put them all on a single visual. That is, don't try to use the same visual image as a key to several different points. Provide a series of different images, with different principal points of focus, though perhaps with common background elements to emphasise the relationship.

144   Chapter 11

For example, Figure 5 shows an overhead-projector transparency that attempted to present several related points. To make those points, the speaker had to leave the same transparency (that is, the same visual image) in front of the audience while talking about different points. For the audience, there was no clear connection between spoken words and visual images.

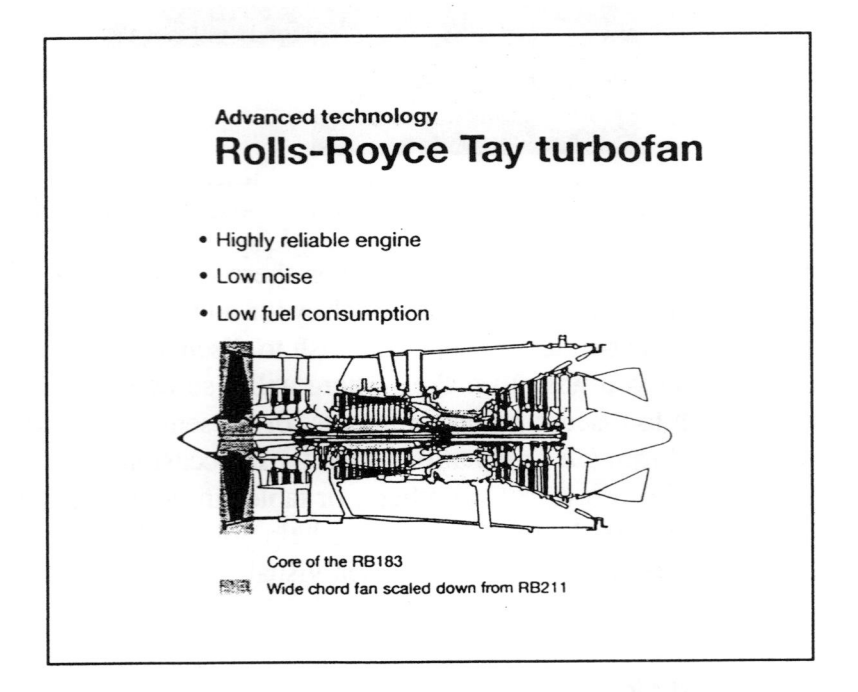

Figure 5. An overloaded OHP transparency, designed to help the speaker make five related points. In fact, it makes only two *points* (about the core and the wide chord fan) and announces three *topics* . This transparency gives the audience little help with focus or recall: the same image is before them while they listen to the speaker's words on five different topics; and though the visual draws attention to specific points about the core and the fan, it gives no help with focusing on or recalling the points made about reliability, noise, or fuel consumption.

Avoiding overload 145

A better effect would have been produced by presenting a separate transparency to give visual emphasis to each point, as is done in the transparencies in Figure 6:

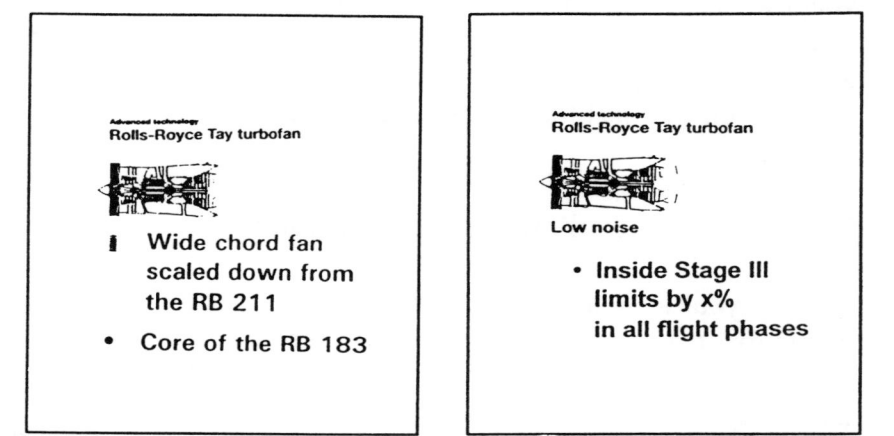

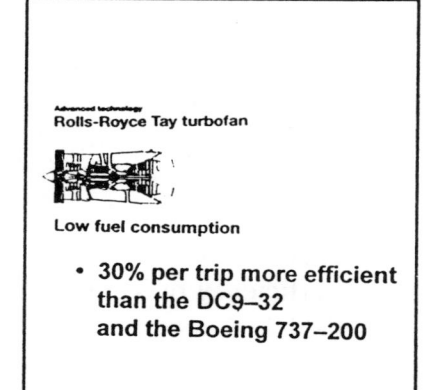

Advanced technology
Rolls-Royce Tay turbofan

- Wide chord fan scaled down from the RB 211
- Core of the RB 183

Advanced technology
Rolls-Royce Tay turbofan

Low noise

- Inside Stage III limits by x% in all flight phases

Advanced technology
Rolls-Royce Tay turbofan

Low fuel consumption

- 30% per trip more efficient than the DC9–32 and the Boeing 737–200

Advanced technology
Rolls-Royce Tay turbofan

High reliability

- Only 5 unplanned removals in more than 1 million in-service flight hours

---

Figure 6. Four overhead transparencies designed to help with focus on and recall of five topics. Repeated elements in the four slides emphasise that the points made are related, but different wording creates different visual images to help the audience with focus and recall.

Figure 6 illustrates another important aspect of the design of 'word visuals'. The words on the transparencies in Figure 6 make *points*: most of the words on Figure 5 simply announce topics. Imagine that you have listened to a lecturer using the transparency in Figure 5. After you have left the lecture room, you ask yourself: 'What point was made about low fuel consumption?' You would get no help with recall from Figure 5: the transparencies in Figure 6 would help you recall the information (not just the topics) presented in the talk.

Meeting your audience's expectations

Meet your audience's expectations about the natural starting points for 'reading' visuals. Normally, readers accustomed to western-style typography will expect to move from top to bottom, left to right, or clockwise. A circular ('pie') chart that requires readers to start reading from the middle of the left-hand side will cause at least momentary confusion.

Remember, too, that readers will decode bar charts or line charts (graphs) in accordance with common conventions. Normally, we interpret the highest bar as signalling the largest value; we interpret a rising line (curve) as representing a sequence of increasing values. The bar chart in Figure 7 confused me for a few moments the first time I saw it. It was introduced to illustrate the superior fuel-efficiency of Vehicle A. At first sight, my impression was that Vehicle C was the most efficient. I assumed that the tallest bar represented the best performance; and that assumption was reinforced by the '+ 30%' written at the top of the bar. It took me a few moments to realise that the dotted line, not the horizontal axis, represented the desirable base line, and that bars extending above that dotted line represented a *worse* performance than that shown by the first bar.

Fuel efficiency

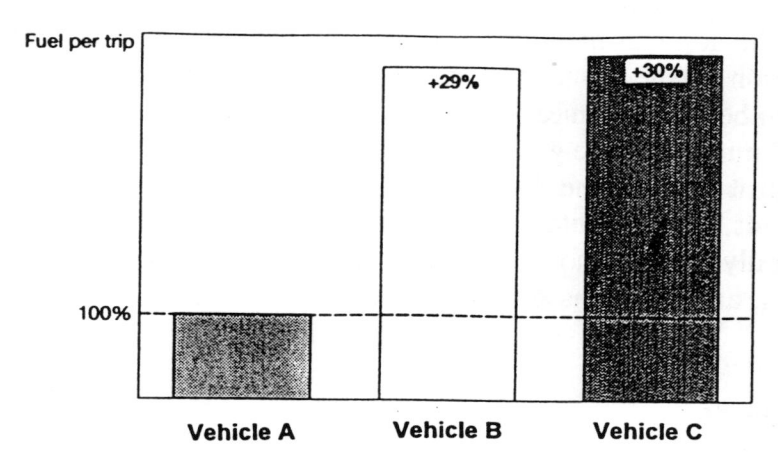

Figure 7. A bar chart that confuses momentarily by departing from the convention that the tallest bar represents the best performance. The design compounds the confusion by adding 'plus 30%' to the apparent fuel efficiency of vehicle C).

As you plan all visuals, make full use of visual cues: spacing, indentation, type styles, shading, and ruling. 'Pull-out' techniques (pulling out and enlarging a small segment of a large picture, chart, or diagram) can help with orientation, focus, and emphasis. Consider using colour to highlight features, and to emphasise connections, comparisons and contrasts. But remember that a few of your audience may be completely colour-blind, and many others may have some difficulty with discrimination between colours and shades. Consider whether you could achieve the same emphasising effect with cues that do not rely on colour alone.

Tables

As visual aids in a presentation, tables are rarely as successful as charts. Tables give numbers: charts make points. Charts *show* what the numbers in tables *imply*. Tables require readers to find certain cells and then make comparisons or associations: in charts, the designer highlights for the audience the comparison or association he/she wants to show. Presentations often require points to be made by means of charts in the main talk, and detailed numbers to be given as handouts after the talk for subsequent scrutiny and discussion. Tables, if used at all as visual aids, should contain only a few rows and columns, should be liberally spaced, should have very clear headings for rows and columns, and should have very clear captions.

Bar charts

Bars can be horizontal, vertical, or 'floating'. In floating bar-charts with horizontal and vertical axes shown, the bars are not attached to either axis. When only a single axis is shown, the bars 'float' across that axis. Floating bar-charts are good for emphasising relative performances:

The bars on bar-charts can be drawn:

- of different heights/lengths, making points by relative height/length;
- all the same height/length, making points by divisions within the bars;
- of different heights/lengths, with subdivision within the bars also, making points by both height/length and width of subdivisions.

Label the tops/ends of bars with significant numbers or labels, to help identification and comparison/contrast.

Avoid dishonest compression (failing to show zero):

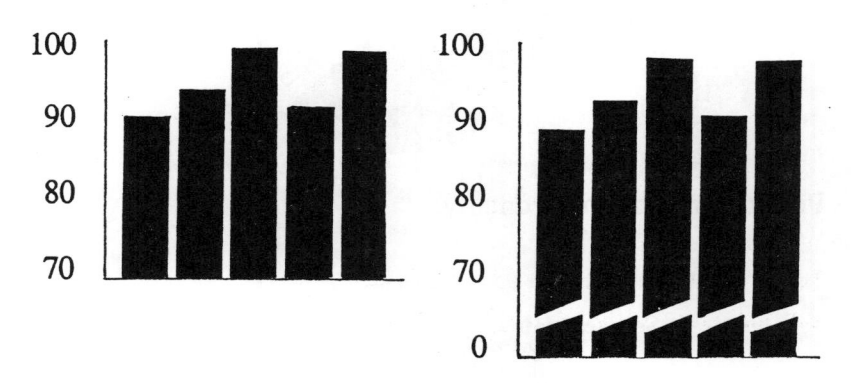

Dishonest compression   Honest compression

150 Chapter 11

Circular ('Pie') charts

Pie charts are good for showing proportions and periodic/cyclic information.

Show the largest (or most significant) proportions at the top, descending clockwise. Focus attention on differences by clearly different hatching. Pull out a segment for extra emphasis.

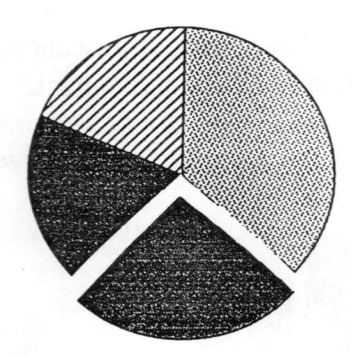

Preferably, label horizontally:

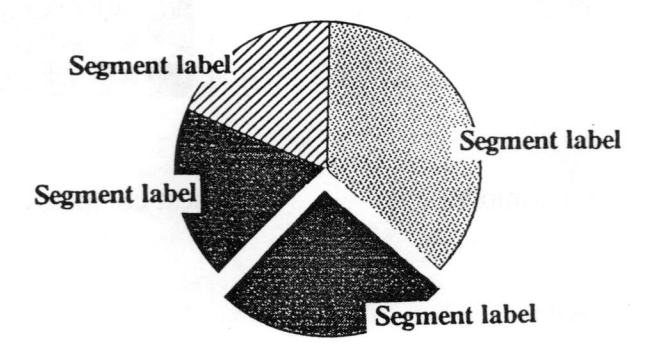

Line charts (graphs)

Choose your scale carefully, so that you show clearly if the line (curve) moves significantly in any direction (a small scale may hide significant movements).

Preferably, do not show more than five lines (curves) on a single chart.

On 'statement' visuals, include on your chart only the minimum number of readings needed to justify your point (perhaps have a full set of readings available to show after the talk to members of the audience who raised questions about your full results).

Background grid lines often make a chart seem too 'busy'. Show only as many grid lines as are necessary to help with quick and accurate reading of the chart.

Label lines (curves) clearly, preferably with words, not with an assortment of asterisks, plus signs, multiplication signs, and other symbols that have to be identified in a key tucked away in a corner of the chart.

Flow charts and block diagrams

Flow charts should emphasise movement, top to bottom, left to right. If possible, keep the movements following from decisions uniform (for example, always YES downwards and NO to the right), although it may sometimes be preferable to give priority to the customary, normal, or most usual flow of decisions.

Rely on flow-chart symbolism (for instance, a rectangle signals a command or an action, a diamond signals a question or decision-point) *only* if you are sure that the symbolism is familiar to your audience. If it is not, ensure that your wording is clear, not mystifyingly cryptic. For example, write 'Do you want to set up X?' or 'Have you set up X?', not just 'Set up X?'.

Block diagrams emphasise relative positions and inter-relationships. If your diagram has to be very detailed, with many blocks and links, try to provide a simplified overview diagram before presenting the details.

CHAPTER 12

Dealing with nervousness

Understanding the causes and effects of nervousness

About 75% of this book is devoted to tactical considerations — preparation, planning, working out what to say and what aids to use. Only about 25% is devoted to the techniques of delivery — the business of actually standing and speaking before the audience.

You may be surprised by these proportions, for as you think about having to give a talk, it is usually the thought of having to *deliver* the talk that makes your blood run cold. It is when you stand before the audience, after all, that you make or break your reputation. If you give a poor performance, the fact that you have prepared thoroughly will count for little with the audience.

This chapter therefore discusses techniques that will help with your presentation. But I want to emphasise that preparation remains the foundation of your performance. The most common comment made to me after courses on speaking can be paraphrased like this: 'I just hadn't realised the extent to which the way you look and feel, and the ease with which the words come, depends on how thoroughly you have prepared your plan of campaign'.

Speakers who are uncertain of what to say are unlikely to be coherent and fluent. If you are incoherent and searching for what to say next, it is likely that you will become uncomfortable and embarrassed. Your discomfiture is likely to be reflected in nervous behaviour — unconscious wringing of hands, sweating, uneasy shifting to and fro. The physical signs of discomfort stem from the lack of preparedness.

Preparedness does not *guarantee* that you feel no physical stress or nervousness during your presentation: but it does remove *un*preparedness as a source of stress and nervousness. That is a very big step in the right direction. It leaves you free to concentrate on dealing with the other sources of stress and nervousness that influence us all.

Does everyone feel nervous about speaking? Most of us do, certainly; and recognising that fact is a step towards reducing your nervousness. If you feel nervous — if you feel increased tension — you are not somehow different, inadequate or abnormal: you are feeling a natural response to a stressful situation. We all feel it: what we have to do is work out what causes the stress — what we are nervous about — then remove as many of the causes as possible, and learn to live with the residue.

Easier said than done? Of course. But it *can* be done, and here are some questions to help with your rationalisation and reduction of your nervousness:

> Why were you asked to speak to a group?
> What are you really afraid of?

Why were you asked to speak to a group?

A common source of nervousness is that speakers feel they have nothing to say. Usually, this is false modesty. Normally, you are asked to speak because you have information or ideas that your audience do not have. Since you possess information or ideas that your listeners do not, you need not be worried about having nothing to say. Certainly, it may not be easy to establish just what level(s) of expertise to assume in your audience, but at least you have a means of starting your preparation: 'What is it that I have to offer that is new?'. If you really have to answer 'Nothing' to that question, then do not speak.

I recognise that, if you are in the academic world, you are sometimes asked to talk simply in order to demonstrate that you can give a talk. You know that your audience know more about the subject than you do. The artificiality in that situation is usually best overcome if you require your assessors to establish at the outset just what assumptions you are to make about the audience's expertise and interests, and the objective you are to simulate for the talk. Assessors who do not make those things clear are making unreasonable — or merely capricious — demands.

What are you really afraid of?

You become nervous because you are afraid of something. What are you afraid of? Physical assault by the audience? Not usually. In general, you are afraid that you will make yourself look foolish, that the audience will react in a disapproving, scornful, irritated or hostile way — that you will let yourself down.

What could lead your audience to disapprove or to feel hostile? That you do not seem to know what you are talking about, that you seem to be wasting their time, that you are confused, incompetent, a charlatan. Your insurance against that is to be thoroughly prepared, with information sensitively chosen and coherently arranged.

Some speakers have told me they are afraid they are going to bore their audiences. If you have that worry, I must ask what you mean when you classify information as 'boring'. If you mean that your material will be 'irrelevant', then you should not present that material anyway. If you mean 'long-winded', keep what you have to say short by giving an incisive statement of the essence of your message, and provide fine detail in another way, not in a talk. I find it hard to believe that material for a talk can be judged both appropriate to the communication task *and* boring. New information that your audience need or will find useful will never be boring. If you have a suspicion that what you plan to present will be uninteresting or not useful — 'boring' — it is likely that it is not appropriate for your talk anyway.

One of the strongest fears is that you will 'dry up': that is, that you will not be able to remember what you wanted to say. Your notes are your insurance against that. Even if you lose track of the point you are on, you can be reassured that you will be able to go on to the next point.

'But what if I recognise the point, but can't find the words to express myself effectively?' The form of your notes should insure against that. As Chapter 7 explained, your notes should contain the essence of your point, not just a title. For example:

NOT: Weaknesses in the existing design

BUT: Existing design weak because:
- too many components
- aluminium in main structure
- welding techniques suspect.

You may also be a little afraid of the symptoms of nervousness themselves, especially if they are severe. They include general weakness, faintness, sweating, palpitation, dryness of mouth. Do these signs mean there is anything wrong with you? Almost certainly not. Reassure yourself by recognising that the symptoms disappear rapidly when the talk is over. Often, they disappear once you get started. Reassure yourself by asking experienced and able speakers if they ever experience any of these symptoms. You will find that most do, or did when they were beginners. They have learned to control them and/or to live with them.

Help yourself, too, by ensuring that you are never physically flustered before you give a talk. Arrive at the venue with time to spare so that you are not literally sweating, out of breath and with pulse racing. Do not take a drink of alcohol to calm yourself down: take a drink of water to help moisten your throat.

Let me assure you that, though you may feel nervous, you will almost certainly look more self-assured than you feel! Time and again, learners who see a video-recording of their first attempt at a presentation remark: 'I don't look as bad as I felt'. That may be only a small comfort, but take that comfort. Possibly you will never come to *enjoy* making presentations; but if you understand the sources of anxiety inherent in speaking to an audience, and learn tactics to deal with them, you have a good chance of becoming well satisfied with the presentations you give.

CHAPTER 13

Delivering the presentation

Doing simple things well

For people who have little or no experience of making presentations, my main advice on delivery is: 'Don't try to do anything clever. Aim at doing simple things well.'.

Standing up straight

Stand up straight. That sounds like a cry from a strict schoolteacher; but it is sound advice for a speaker. It does not mean that you must pull yourself up with a guardsman's rigidity: it *does* mean that you should stand with your weight distributed evenly on both feet, facing the audience squarely, so that your straight-ahead view will keep you comfortably in eye-contact with most of your audience:

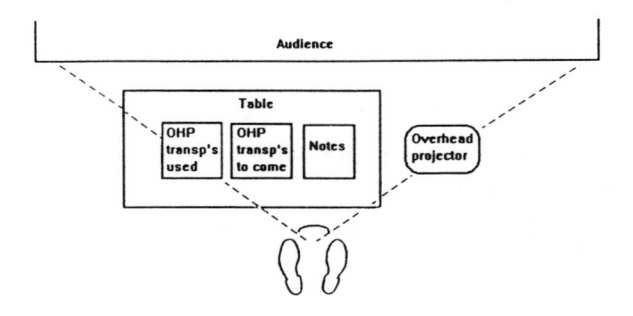

If you allow your weight to drop back mainly on to one foot, it is probable that your body will turn slightly (with your right shoulder back if your right foot moves back), and your straight-ahead view will no longer span most of the audience comfortably:

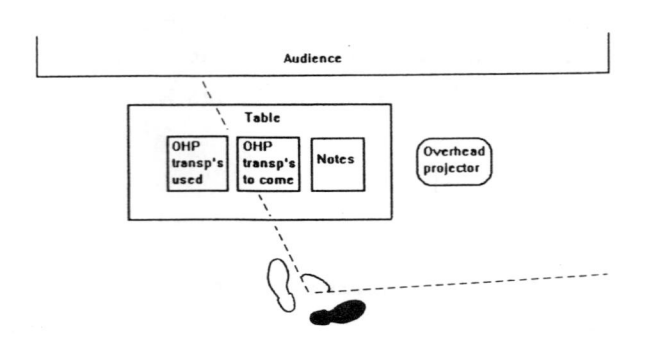

Of course, you can deliberately turn your head to stay in touch with the part of your audience outside your straight-ahead view; but because maintaining contact with that part of the audience requires a distinct turn of the head, not just a movement of the eyes, many speakers consciously or unconsciously abandon that contact. Consequently, part of the audience feels ignored, and the quality of the interaction over-all is reduced.

If you allow your weight to drop back mainly on to one foot, it is probable, too, that your stance will look off-hand or droopy. It is easy to slip over the fine line between looking relaxed and looking uninterested. You want to seem interested and involved, so stand comfortably before your audience, talking directly to them.

What to do with your hands

'What should I do with my hands?' That is a frequent question from inexperienced speakers. In general, my advice is that you should let your hands look after themselves. Most of us gesture unconsciously when we are speaking, some of us more than others. When we try to gesture more than usual or less than usual, our efforts look artificial. It is best to aim to be as natural as possible without being distracting.

It is unnatural to stand motionless, with your arms straight down at your sides. It is unnatural, too, to move your arms perpetually. So don't try to be unnaturally still or unnaturally animated. There is no need to adopt special postures or make special gestures during presentations.

Gradually, as you become more experienced, you will find that you are able to pay more attention to refinements of posture and gesture. At first, however, simply avoid getting stuck in one posture or making the same gesture repeatedly. There is a wide range of natural postures: arms folded; hands clasped behind your back; clasping one wrist with the other hand; leaning with one or both hands on the table; ... . It is not natural, though, to adopt just one posture for 10, 20, or 50 minutes. Similarly, there is a wide range of natural gestures, but it is not natural to make the same gesture over and over again. So during your presentation, change your posture from time to time; also, gesture freely, but not perpetually or repetitively.

Movement

It is natural and helpful to 'punctuate' your talk with movement. Watch people who are talking to one another. You will see how their movements frequently complement the stages in their conversation. Your audience will find it natural and comfortable if you do the same.

Move, but don't shift to and fro restlessly. If you are using visual-aid equipment, your natural movement between your table and the display surface will punctuate your talk helpfully. If you are not using equipment, but are simply standing at your table, plan to move occasionally a little to the left or a little to the right as you progress from point to point. This is not to suggest that you should stray too far from your notes, or that you should shuttle mechanically from side to side. My suggestion is aimed at helping you seem animated. It is to invite you to recognise the distraction caused by a restless speaker, and the apparent lifelessness of one who remains motionless.

Speaking comprehensibly and clearly

As listeners, we want a speaker to be easy to understand and easy to listen to. The ease with which we can understand is affected by two factors: the skill with which the information has been selected and arranged, and the skill with which language has been chosen to express the information. The ease with which we can listen is affected by how the speaker uses his/her voice, and by his/her demeanour during the presentation.

Chapters 2 to 6 have focused on selecting and tailoring information to the needs, interests, and capacities of the audience, and the first part of this chapter has been concerned with general demeanour — posture, gesture, and movement. The following six sections discuss choice of language and qualities of speech.

Over-all policy for choosing language

My advice on language can be summed up succinctly: speak as simply and naturally as possible. That is, keep specialist vocabulary to a minimum, use 'plain English' wherever possible ('plain English' meaning uncomplicated sentences and familiar vocabulary), and keep your voice as varied and animated as possible.

Use of jargon

In most technical, commercial, or administrative presentations, you will have to use jargon — the specialist terminology of a subject or activity. But use of jargon usually makes a presentation seem heavily formal, so although your audience may understand it, keep it to a minimum.

The time to decide which items of jargon are essential is during the selection of material for your talk. It is vital to estimate which of the essential items of jargon will be familiar to *all* your audience, which items will have to be explained, and how long any explanation will take.

Plan each explanation carefully. Consider giving your audience visual help with learning important new terms or expressions. Perhaps plan to put a definition on a blackboard or flip-chart. Perhaps have a flip-chart prepared in advance. If you are using an overhead projector, perhaps have an extra transparency ready with a definition; but if you have only one OHP, it may be better to put your definition on a blackboard or flip-chart so that the definition can remain available in the background while you continue your presentation.

'Plain English'

Resist the temptation to adopt a special 'public speaking' mode of expression. Are *you* impressed by speakers who adopt a formal, oratorical mode of expression, full of elaborate statements, and loaded with 'scholarly' vocabulary? Most of us are not. Most of us admire speakers who seem to be able to reduce complex ideas to simple statements expressed mainly in everyday terms. So, resist the temptation to say:

> It is a matter for conjecture as to the reason for this eventuality but I will hypothesise at this early stage that it will be found to be attributable to ...

(I'm sorry to say that utterance is a quotation: I did not invent it!) Prefer:

> We do not know what is causing this problem, but I suspect it is caused by ...

or:

> We can only guess at the cause of this problem. My guess is that ...

Speaking to multi-national audiences

Plan carefully the language you will use, and listen to yourself as you speak, judging carefully the difficulty *for the audience* of each sentence you produce. Especially, if some of your audience are not native speakers of English, constant monitoring of your expression is vital.

You may have planned to avoid expressions that might be too difficult for some of the audience; but when you are in full flow

Speaking to multi-national audiences 165

in the middle of your presentation, it is easy to slip into language that may be incomprehensible to some of your listeners. Even single words can cause trouble, sometimes because they have two or more meanings, and sometimes because they are used relatively rarely in everyday conversation, and therefore are not within the command of even experienced listeners from overseas:

> 'If you *spot* any irregularities ...'
> '... the ABC program. *Once* installed and running with the XYZ program, ...'
> '*Empowered* with the X workgroup cluster, your design team can focus ...'

Colloquial idioms, in particular, must be avoided:

> 'We *got a lot of stick* from our customers because ...'
> 'We feel that Company X *has the edge* in designing precalciner systems.'
> '... ratio was 0.9:1, which we thought was *rather steep* considering ...'

Beware of sporting idioms. You may think that golf is an international game, but will your audience understand the expression: '... that weekly profit was *par for the course*'? Of course, British speakers must avoid allusions to cricket ('We *hit them for six* ...'), and American speakers must avoid allusions to baseball ('I just wanted *to touch base* with you on ...).

If possible, find out about 'false friends' — words that appear in English and in other languages, but have different meanings in the other languages. For example, *actuel* in French looks like English *actual*. In fact, it means 'present, current'. Some words even have different meanings in British English and American English. This statement from a speaker of American English meant that supplements should be taken with 'normal' or 'usual' food:

> In cases where the patient cannot eat enough,
> liquid supplements taken with *regular* food will
> provide the calories and protein required.

As a speaker of British English, I assumed that 'regular' food meant food taken at uniform intervals — a very different idea.

It is well-nigh impossible to learn all the false friends that exist among languages. The best you can do is gradually build your own list of expressions to avoid. Also, if at all possible, rehearse your presentation in front of one or more friends or colleagues, and ask them if they can foresee that the language you have chosen will create problems for multi-national audiences. (A detailed discussion of writing for multi-national audiences is available in my chapter 'How Friendly is your Writing for Readers Around the World?', in **Text, Context and Hypertext**, edited by Edward Barrett, MIT Press, 1987, pages 343–364.)

'Fillers'

Minimise your indulgence in 'fillers' — *um, er, you know, well, sort of,* ... . Let me say at once that it is unlikely that you will be able to speak without some of those meaningless noises, and that you should not concentrate too much attention on eradicating them while you are a beginner at public speaking. We all use them occasionally in day-to-day speech. But when they occur frequently, they become a distraction: instead of concentrating on your message, your listeners begin to count the *um*s! Listen to yourself as you talk. If possible, make recordings of your rehearsals and presentations, so that you can review your performances. Gradually, as you become more experienced, and you are able to attend to such matters of detail, remove any irritating voice mannerisms from your delivery.

Clarity of diction and variety of intonation

If you are an experienced attender at meetings, you will know that loudness of speech is not all that matters to the listener: clarity of diction is just as important.

When you arrive in your lecture-room, look at the back row of the audience, and judge how much you will need to raise your voice to enable them to hear easily. But judge carefully: to become *too* loud will seem hectoring and exhausting.

Articulate clearly. The most frequent cause of apologies such as 'Sorry, I didn't catch that' is speech that is too rapid or indistinct. So speak carefully — not with a special, affected voice, but making sure that each word can be heard distinctly. Remember that *you* know what you intended to say, and you are very familiar with your usual rate and manner of speech: listeners will probably welcome a slightly slower delivery than *you* find comfortable, at least for the first few minutes of your talk, while they 'tune in' to your voice and manner.

It is difficult to judge the clarity and speed of your own speech. When you begin to make presentations (and from time to time afterwards), ask a few friends to tell you how the clarity and speed of your speech compares with another mutual friend's. That should help you judge whether or not you need to make adjustments for the benefit of your audiences.

Speak with varied stress and intonation. In presentations, speakers are often so busy concentrating on the technicalities of their subject-matter that they allow their speech to degenerate to an expressionless monotone. A single-tone (monotonous) output is boring to listen to.

In everyday conversation, we make great use of variations of stress and intonation, not only to signal meaning but also to show our involvement in what we are saying. For example, imagine yourself saying: 'Would you rather *I* cut your hair, or would you rather have it cut at a hairdresser's?'. You will notice that you put extra stress on *I*, that you use a rising intonation as you say '... *I* cut your hair, ...', and that your intonation drops as you come towards the end of the sentence: '... have it cut professionally?'. Your variations of stress and intonation give vitality — perhaps just a querying tone, or perhaps a flavour of challenge — to those words. If you had been using them in real life, they would have shown your interest in the question you were asking. Aim to get similar vitality and indication of interest in your presentations. Think of your talks as a 'loud conversations' with your audience. Of course, a presentation is not the same type of interaction as a conversation: your 'interlocutors' normally remain silent; but your task is still to involve them in your flow of thought, to ensure that they understand what you are telling them — to interact with them. If you think of your presentation as an interaction, you have a good chance of retaining the lively rhythms and varied intonation of conversation; if you think of your task as simply 'speaking in front of an audience', it is likely that your delivery will become 'flat' — that you will think of the activity as simply one of giving out, not of giving and receiving, and you will lose variations of stress and intonation that usually accompany the ebb and flow of exchange.

Maintaining eye-contact

Good eye-contact is vital to effective interaction. In Chapter 10, I suggested that the position you adopt during handling of visual-aid equipment should enable you to maintain good eye-contact. In this chapter, I have suggested that your stance at your table or lectern should also enable you to maintain good eye-contact. If you cannot look into the eyes of your audience, you have little chance of judging accurately how well your presentation is being understood and accepted. (That is a powerful argument against choosing to use any visual-aid equipment that requires the lecture-room lighting to be dimmed or switched off.)

Look steadily from person to person in your audience as you speak. You will learn from experience how quickly to move from one person to another: to move too quickly may create an evasive impression; to gaze for too long may cause embarrassment! As an inexperienced speaker, you may be tempted to avoid difficulties by not looking at the audience at all! In addition to losing feedback, you will lose goodwill. If you have been in an audience in front of a speaker who has looked everywhere but at you, you will know how discourteous the speaker's lack of contact can seem.

Level of formality

It is essential to judge accurately the level of formality suitable to the interaction between yourself and the audience. In what you say and how you say it, beware of seeming distant or disdainful; but equally, avoid seeming presumptuously casual. Be serious, not solemn; be friendly, not over-familiar. Concentrate on being simple, clear, straightforward, and courteous: *any* attempt at a special tone, either particularly light-hearted or particularly serious, will open up the possibility that somebody will judge you unfavourably.

In particular, resist the temptation to introduce humour, especially for multi-national audiences.

It is a mistake to think that being friendly necessarily involves making jokes, or that being informal necessarily involves being casual or slangy. Friendliness and informality lie in being open, helpful, easy to understand, and pleasant in demeanour.

Notions of what is humorous, and when it is appropriate to be humorous, vary from group to group, country to country, and culture to culture. Audiences may feel that humour is not appropriate to the topic you are discussing; they may consider that humour is inappropriate for an audience such as themselves (especially if you are a junior addressing seniors); or they may feel that humour is out of place at the time and in the context in which you are speaking. Typical British irony or under-statement may simply not be recognised, let alone understood or found amusing, by listeners for whom English is a second language.

I recommend, therefore, that you resist the temptation to introduce jokes, or even to allow yourself light-hearted 'asides', unless you are absolutely confident that all your audience have the same sense of humour as you have.

Dealing with questions

Careful judgement of tone is especially important when you are dealing with questions. Be careful not to sound impatient, or as if you wish you had not been asked!

Questioners are not always trying to trip you up. A questioner simply may not have heard a word or two of your argument, or may simply want to be reassured that he or she has comprehended correctly what you have said. Even if you do detect that a questioner's intention is hostile, be unfailingly patient, though not condescendingly so.

In all but the smallest meetings (and sometimes in them, too), before you answer a question, repeat it. This has two purposes: to demonstrate that you have heard the question correctly; and to ensure that all the audience have heard what you have been asked, and so can remain involved. (You also gain a little time for thinking of your answer!)

Answer succinctly but clearly. Answer especially succinctly if the question plainly arises from the questioner only — you can see from the faces of the rest of the audience that they do not need an answer to that question. You should not direct all your attention to a single member of the audience for too long; but you must answer adequately, because the rest of the audience will be judging your answer as part of their judgement of your overall competence.

Be polite, even to an aggressive questioner. Normally, the audience will be on your side if a questioner seems harsh or unreasonably persistent; but if you lose patience and are abrupt or rude, you will be considered to have broken the rules of good behaviour as badly as the questioner.

Don't allow a single member of your audience to monopolise your attention, either aggressively, or out of genuine enthusiasm. If the audience begin to lose interest in the questions you are being asked (you will recognise the common signals, from noisy closing of books, to the beginning of local conversations!), invite the questioner to talk to you after the presentation. But be careful not to seem abrupt; and use careful wording, so that you do not seem to exclude other members of the audience from the continuing discussions:

> ... Perhaps we should continue our discussion of that point during the coffee break, because it is taking us away from our main discussion of X; but I hope other members of the audience will join us if they, too, would like to follow up that point further.

Rehearsing

Try to find time and space for a rehearsal before every presentation. Rehearsing does not necessarily mean full-scale presentation in a lecture-room, although it is valuable if you can manage that. The essence of rehearsing is that you go right through your presentation, speaking the words and handling the visuals as though you were participating in the event itself. It is possible to do this with just one helpful colleague, or even by yourself.

If you can find a helpful colleague, sit face to face, and simulate the presentation as closely as possible. Speak as you would do to your audience, and hold up your visual materials so that he or she can see them. Do NOT be satisfied with saying: 'At this point, I shall introduce this topic or this visual.'. Practise finding the words you will need; simulate putting your transparency on the overhead projector, recognising not only what you will want to say about it but also how much time will be taken by manipulation of the machine; adjust your notes, if necessary, to remind yourself to leave the projector switched on because the next transparency is due in a few seconds, or remind yourself to switch it off because you will have finished with it for a few minutes.

Ask for your colleague's views not only on your delivery of the presentation but also on its content. The word *rehearse* is derived from a word meaning 'to harrow', and that notion — of breaking up chunks, turning things over, refining, smoothing — is a good one to have in mind as you think through your presentation.

As I urged in Chapter 10, try to foresee every move you will have to make in your presentation. Of course, if you accept questions during your talk, you will not be able to foresee precisely what will arise; but at least consider in advance whether or not you will accept questions. If you will not, think out a polite wording with which to tell your audience *in advance* (not in an apparently hasty evasion at the first sound of a query) that you would prefer them to hold questions until a specified point in your presentation. Preferably, give a reason for such a request (such as the need to explain fully one part of your case before another part can be understood satisfactorily). Always sound willing to receive questions: apparent reluctance breeds suspicion.

If you *will* be prepared to accept questions during the talk, try to forecast what they will be. Ask your helpful colleague to look deliberately for loopholes in your case or uncertainties that might arise in your audience's minds as they listen to your account. A colleague's lines of thought will almost certainly be different from the lines along which you have been thinking during the preparation of your presentation, and he or she may spot unexplained assumptions or unnecessary details that you have failed to recognise.

It is a sign of confidence, not an admission of weakness, to acknowledge that someone else may be able to see ways in which your plan of campaign might be improved. Always listen carefully to criticism; but then, always take the final decision on what to say or not to say *yourself*. *You* are the person who has to stand before the audience; *you* are the person who is going to feel rueful if someone else's advice turns out to be wrong; *you* are the person who is going to feel very satisfied if all your judgements turn out to be well founded!

Preparing a 'Plan B'

In Chapter 7, pages 60–63, I urged you to be prepared to adjust your plan of campaign in the event of a late start or over-running by previous speakers. I should like to repeat that warning as a postscript to this chapter on delivery.

Consider, for example, what you will do if, during the delivery of your talk, you are interrupted many times, and it becomes obvious that you cannot reasonably cover all that you had planned to cover. Work out in advance what you will leave out, and/or where you will stop, if the need arises. Experienced speakers always have a 'Plan B' — an emergency plan, not only for what to do if they are running out of time, but also for what to do if the projector bulb fails or if the power is cut off altogether!

To have a Plan B is especially important if you are to make a presentation away from your home base. I recommend that you always have enough handout material to enable you to survive without overhead transparencies or other aids. You probably need not have the whole of your back-up material in handout form: take just enough to be able to present a clear nucleus or the principal points of your talk.

If you are new to the task of making presentations, you may feel that you have enough to think about in preparing a Plan A, without having to prepare a Plan B! Nevertheless, I commend to you the reassuring feeling of having prepared for just about every eventuality you can foresee. A policy of trying to foresee everything has helped me to survive through a long career as a speaker. I have even come to enjoy the challenge of making presentations! Perhaps, one day, you will do so, too.

APPENDIX

Check-lists for evaluating presentations

If you are asked to evaluate a presentation, the following check-lists will help you remember what to consider.

The same lists will help you during the preparation of your own presentations, by reminding you of the things you ought to have considered.

Criteria related to content

Selection

- Was the topic chosen well suited to the time, place, 'mood of the moment ', ... ?

- Was the material included well suited to the speaker's intention (which may have been to teach/interest/amuse/explore/persuade/.....)?

- Was the material included well suited to the audience's:
    - needs
    - interests
    - level of technical expertise
    - level of linguistic expertise?

Organisation

- Did the speaker catch and hold interest at the start?

- Did the speaker provide orientation for the audience by establishing at the outset (if necessary) his/her credentials, reason for speaking, and plan for the ensuing talk?

- Was the middle of the talk constructed coherently, with judicious inter-mixing of description and explanation, fact and opinion, new information and example, outline and detail, assertion and evidence?

- Was new material linked to the audience's experience by the use of example, analogy, careful transitions?

- Was any of the material emotionally charged, and if so, was it introduced at strategic points and in shrewd terms, so that disturbance or hostile response from the audience was avoided?

- Was the ending effective? Did it leave a sense of completed discourse? Was it a suitable culmination from the points of view both of information and courtesy to the audience?

Unloading

- Was the information unloaded at a rate appropriate to the audience's:
    - intellectual capacity
    - psychological readiness?

- Did the speaker provide reiteration and reinforcement (especially if the objective was for the audience to *learn* the information)?

Criteria related to delivery

Demeanour

- Physical appearance. Was the speaker's dress and grooming appropriate to the occasion?

- Emotional appearance. Did the speaker seem:
    - enthusiastic/bored
    - friendly/patronising
    - animated/lifeless
    - confident/terrified?

- Posture. Did the speaker's stance and general movement seem comfortable?

- Gesture. Did the speaker gesture comfortably, naturally, and with variation?

- Courtesy. Did the speaker exercise patience and self-control in dealing with questions? Was the over-all tone appropriate, or was it condescending/lecturing/hectoring/plaintive/whining/..... ?

- Confidence/authority. Did the speaker instil confidence by his/her own apparent confidence, by obvious organisation and preparedness, and by ready expression of ideas and information?

Technique

- Voice: - Was volume suitable to the size of the room?
    - Was diction clear or slurred?
    - Was intonation varied or monotonous?
    - Was tone harsh/strident/soothing/friendly/..... ?

- Was stress varied ?
- Was dialect a barrier to comprehension?

- Fluency. Was delivery at an acceptable rate? Was pace varied? Was hesitancy (and use of 'fillers') a disturbance to the audience's attention?

- Eye contact. Did the speaker talk to the audience or avoid eye contact?

- Notes. Did the speaker handle his/her notes unobtrusively?

- Feedback. Did the speaker seem sensitive to the audience's response, as shown by adjustments of pace, tone, and language?

- Visual aids.
  - Were the speaker's visual materials (transparencies, charts, etc) well designed?
  - Were they legible?
  - Was the purpose of each visual clear?
  - Did the speaker co-ordinate words and visuals skilfully, usually leading with words, and ensuring that words and images matched at all times?
  - Did the speaker handle the visual-aid equipment confidently and smoothly?
  - Did the speaker position himself/herself wisely while using the visual-aid equipment, maintaining eye-contact with the audience, and leaving the audience's sight-lines clear at all times?

INDEX

abstractions, visual aids to help present 71
academic situations, v. real-life situations 7
aim, analysing 7–9
analysing aim 7–9
analysing audience 9–12
analysing context 12–14
anecdote, beginning with 32–33
arrow torch 130
assembling material 15
assertion, beginning with 32
atmosphere among audience 12
attention
    catching and holding 16, 25–29, 32–35
    definition of 22
attitudes of audience 12
audience
    analysing 9–12
    atmosphere 12
    attitudes 12
    awareness 12
    expectations 11, 12
    expertise 11
    interests 11
    mix 11
    motivation 11, 22
    needs 11
    responses 9
audio aids 121–122
awareness of audience 12

bad news, presenting 25
bar charts 146, 148–149
beginning
    time to allocate to 37–38
    with a story or assertion 32
beliefs of audience 12

block diagrams 151–152
British humour 170

captions on visual images 73
catching and holding attention 16, 25–29, 32–35
chalkboards 85–87
charts
    bar 146
    circular (pie) 150
    flow 151
    line (graph) 151
clarity of diction 167–168
closed-circuit television 120–121
colleague as helper 131
colour, use of in visuals 147
colloquialisms 165
command of the subject 4
communication tasks, possible 9
compression, dishonest 149
conclusion of a talk 47–49
context, analysing 14
controlling reading of visuals 140–141
co-ordination 1
credentials, establishing your 29
cues, visual 147
cultural differences 170
curiosity, playing on 32

delivery, speed of 43
describing, strategy for 41–43
designing visual material 137–152
diagrams 94–96, 151–152
diction, clarity of 167–168
drafting 17
drying up 156

Index

elocution 4
ending
 bringing a talk to an 47–49
 time to allocate to 37–38
English, standard accent 4
English, plain 163, 164
Envisioning Information 137
er 166
establishing your credentials 29
expectations, of audience 11, 12
expectations of the audience,
 reading visuals 146–147
expertise, of audience 11, 12
explaining, strategy for 41–43
extemporising 51–52
eye contact 56, 126–127, 168–169

false friends 165–166
feedback
 from other learners 3
 from your audience 57
fillers 166
film loops 117–118
films 117–118
film-strips 117–118
flip-charts 87–88
floating bar charts 148–149
flow charts 151–152
focus
 division of 102
 visual material to help 137
formality, level of 169

gestures 161
good start, getting a 21
graphs 151
guessing, keeping the audience 32

handouts 98–112
hands, what to do with them 161

helper, colleague as 131
holding attention 16
holding notes 66
humour 33, 169–170

ideas, stimulating 17
idioms 165
illustration visuals 138
information, shape and pattern of 18
interaction, presentation as 10
interests of audience 11
intonation, variety of 167–168
irony 170

jargon 163

keeping the audience guessing 32

labelling bar charts 149
language, over-all policy for 163
late start, planning for 61–63
leading with words 131–133, 140
level of formality 169
line charts (graphs) 151
lines of sight, for audience 13, 18
long-term memory 44–45

'mix', of audience 11
main body of the talk, organising 38–46
mannerisms of voice 167
maps and plans 94–96
meeting the audience's expectations 146–147
memory, short-term and long-term 44–45

mismatch of words and images 134–135
mode of presentation, varying 74
motivation
 aiding 23, 26
 definition of 22
motivation of audience 11
movement 161–162
multi-media 122
multi-national audiences 164–166, 169–170

needs of audience 11
nervousness, dealing with 153–157
notes
 form of 156
 holding 66
 in outlining 17
 length of 63
 preparing 51–68
 size and layout of 64
 using visual aids as 53–54
numbers
 presenting 70
 visual impact of 141–143

'obvious' structures 15–16
objects and processes, visual aids to help present 70–71
on-the-spot creation of visuals 82–84
organising the main body of the talk 38–46
orientation
 aiding 31
 definition of 23
 statement 132
outlining 15–18
overhead projectors 89–94
overload, visual 143–146

pattern of information 18, 31, 143
persuasion 13
photographs 94–96
physical models 96–98
pie charts 150
plain English 163, 164
plan B, preparing 173–174
playing on the audience's curiosity 32
pointing 129–131, 141
position to stand in 126–129
posture 161
practice 2
prepared large-scale sheets 94–96
presenting bad news 25
projectors, overhead 89–94
projectors, 35mm slide 112–116
pull-out techniques 147

question and answer session 12
questions, dealing with 169–170

rapport, establishing 115, 119
reading a script 55–58
real-life situations v. academic situations 7
rehearsal 22, 171–173
reinforcing your message, visual aids for 75
reluctant audience, dealing with 23
relying on stereotypes 10
responses, audience 9

samples as visual aids 96–98
scale, on graphs 151
script, using a full 55–58
selecting 8
self-appraisal 3

Index

shape of information 18, 31, 143
short-term memory 44–45
sight, lines of 13, 18
slide projectors 112–116
speed of delivery 43
speed of speech 167
standard English 4
standing position 126–129
standing up straight 56, 159–161
start, getting a good 21–36
starting late, planning for 61–63, 173–174
statement visuals 138
stereotypes, relying on 10
stimulating ideas 17
story, beginning with 32
stress 2, 154
structures, possible 39–40
summary, at start 16
synchronising words with visuals 77

tables 148
tasks, possible communication 9
thinking through 58, 123
time
    available 13
    deciding proportions of 37–38
    indications in notes 59–60
    of day for the presentation 13
torch, arrow 130
transparencies, design of 93
Tufte, Edward 137

um 166
understanding of the situation 12
understatement 170
unloading rate 43

values of audience 12
varying mode of presentation 74
venue for the presentation 12, 13, 81, 123–125
verbal frame for visual images 72
videotapes as visual aids 118–120
visual-aid equipment
    advantages and disadvantages of common types 84–122
    handling 123–135
    using more than one type 84
visual aids
    audio aids 121–122
    chalkboards 85–87
    closed-circuit television 120–121
    creating on the spot 82–84
    deciding whether to use 69–78
    deciding which to use 79–122
    films 117–118
    film strips 117–118
    flip-charts 87–88
    for presenting abstractions 71
    for presenting numbers 70
    for presenting objects and processes 70
    for reinforcing your message 75
    handouts 98–112
    in the selection process 46
    maps 94–96
    multi-media 122
    overhead projectors 89–94
    photographs 94–96
    physical models 96–98
    prepared large-scale sheets 94–96
    reminders in your notes 58
    samples 96–98
    slide projectors 112–116
    using as notes 53–54

using throughout a presentation 76
   videotapes 118–120
visual cues 147
Visual Display of Quantitative Information 137
visual images
   synchronising with words 77
   verbal frame for 72
visual material
   designing 137–152
   to help focusing 137
   to help remembering 137
visual overload 143–146

whiteboards 85–87
'Wimbledon spectator position' 126, 129
word:image mismatching 134–135, 140
words, visual impact of 141–143